FOR THOSE WHO DO NOT BELIEVE IN MIRACLES

*The resilience of a
Rwandan woman
who survived the genocide*

Mama Lambert and Hans Dekkers

WOLF LEGAL PUBLISHERS

FOR THOSE WHO DO NOT BELIEVE IN MIRACLES

The resilience of a Rwandan woman who survived the genocide

Mama Lambert and Hans Dekkers

ISBN: 9789462402713

Published by:
Wolf Legal Publishers (WLP)
Postbus 313
5060 AH Oisterwijk
info@wolfpublishers.nl
www.wolfpublishers.com

All rights reserved. No part of this publication may be reproduced, stored in a retrieval system, or transmitted in any form or by any means, electronic, mechanical, photocopying, recording or otherwise, without prior written permission of the publisher. Whilst the authors, editors and publisher have tried to ensure the accuracy of this publication, the publisher, authors and editors cannot accept responsibility for any errors, omissions, misstatements, or mistakes and accept no responsibility for the use of the information presented in this work.

© Mama Lambert and Hans Dekkers / WLP 2015
© Translated from Dutch: Mama Lambert en Hans Dekkers, *Voor wie niet in wonderen gelooft: De veerkracht van een Rwandese vrouw die de genocide overleefde* (WLP 2015).

This book is dedicated to:

My children:
Dieudonné Rucyahana, Denise Mwenedata and Lambert Nkurunziza.
My nephews and nieces: Donatien Munyarubuga, Eugenie Niyonsaba,
Françoise Mukamana and Francine Biziyesu.
Two of my daughter Claudette's good friends:
Frida Umuhoza and Sophie Umuhire.
And everyone who miraculously survived the genocide
against the Tutsis in 1994.

In memory of:

My dear husband: Placide Rucyahana.
My dear children: Germaine Uwishimye, Claudette Umugwaneza,
Germain Busoro Micomyiza, Olivier Mugisha, John Rutayisire Bébé.
My parents: Eliezer Gakwaya and Maria Mukakimenyi.
My parents-in-law: Jean Baptiste Gafaranga and Annonciata Mutumwinka.
My brother and sister: Elias Munyarubuga and Rosalie Mukankubito.
My brother-in-law and sister-in-law: Valens Ntaganda and
Placidie Nyinawankusi.
My uncles, aunts, cousins and neighbours.
And all victims murdered during the genocide against the Tutsis.

"I believe we will see one another again in heaven."

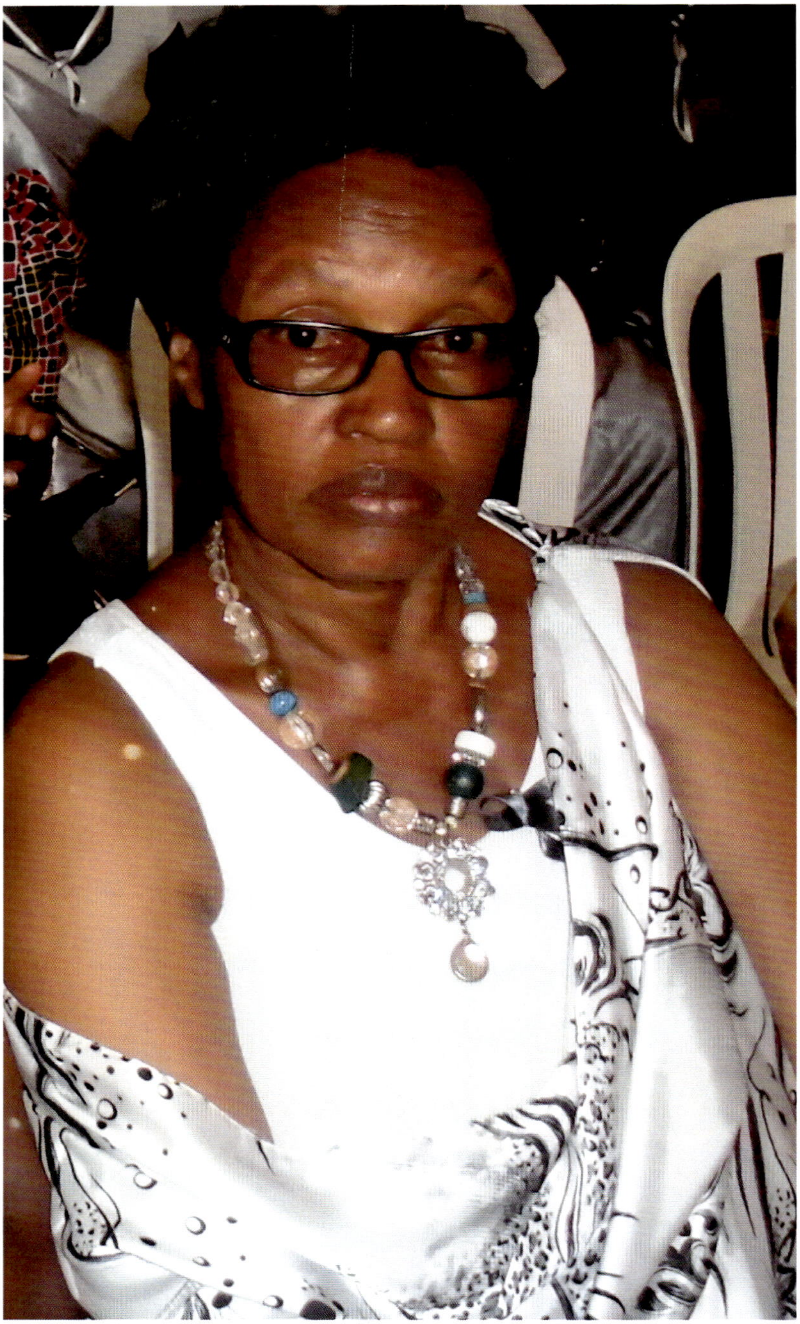

FOREWORD

The subject of women and conflict is becoming increasingly prominent in the daily news. Hundreds of women and girls are trafficked in slave markets by the so-called Islamic State, Nigerian school girls are abducted, and Syrian women inexplicably disappear. However, this phenomenon is not confined to recent times. Mama Lambert reflects on the 1994 Rwandan genocide, when more than 400,000 women and girls were raped by Hutu extremists.

Thanks to the actions of Swedish politician Margot Wallström, the UN Special Representative on Sexual Violence in Conflict since 2010, rape now has the status of a 'strategic weapon', because it is intentionally deployed to destroy communities. This weapon tears apart and profoundly demoralises families and communities.

War and conflict are coupled with loss, including loss of safety, loss of family, loss of dignity and self-esteem, loss of the most basic materials for survival, and loss of dreams. In Rwanda not only did one million people lose their lives, but those who survived also lost their cattle, a status symbol and important source of food in Rwanda. They were left completely destitute and broken.

During my activities for the Dutch Council for Refugees, UNICEF, Vrouwen van Nu (Women of Today) and as Dutch Women's Representative to the General Assembly of the UN in 2012, I have come into contact with thousands of women and girls who have been victims of war and conflict. They struggle with a multitude of consequences. These women often go in search of safety and support abroad, a course of action that always comes with grief, fear, pain, rage, uncertainty and feelings of guilt. Mama Lambert takes her own path. She does not flee from Rwanda or her past, instead looking the murderers and her trauma straight in the eye.

Mama Lambert's voice rings loud and clear through this book. Her story is unimaginable to us. Her parents, her husband, five of her eight children, a brother, sister, and countless other family members were murdered. With no possessions and her one-year-old son Lambert on her back, she fled into the woods and swamps, seriously traumatised, bereft of almost everything she had and with nothing more to give. Miraculously, mother and child manage to survive for three months.

The story of Mama Lambert is particularly special for the way in which she deals with her trauma. Realising that she cannot continue her life as before, she forgives those who murdered. With the help of the organisation Solace Ministries, she worked on her trauma until she felt willing and able to help others through her experience. The Dutch Mukomeze Foundation, led by a committed woman, has made it possible for those of us in the Netherlands and elsewhere to be inspired by Mama Lambert and her story.

It is often women who ensure that initiatives are taken after a war or conflict to get a shattered society back on its feet. As a trauma therapist for Solace Ministries, Mama Lambert works day-in and day-out to inspire women as well as men not to give up but to find a new aim in life. This allows her to heal herself, the affected population and the torn country.

Mama Lambert finds so much strength and inspiration in forgiveness that there is plenty for others to draw on, including you and me. Mama Lambert teaches us that forgiveness takes us from beaten to unbeatable.

As women we make up half the world, so I would like to pass on the message to those who are oppressed, abused and exploited on a large scale.

Anke Vervoord, Director of Vrouwen van Nu (Women of Today)

RWANDA

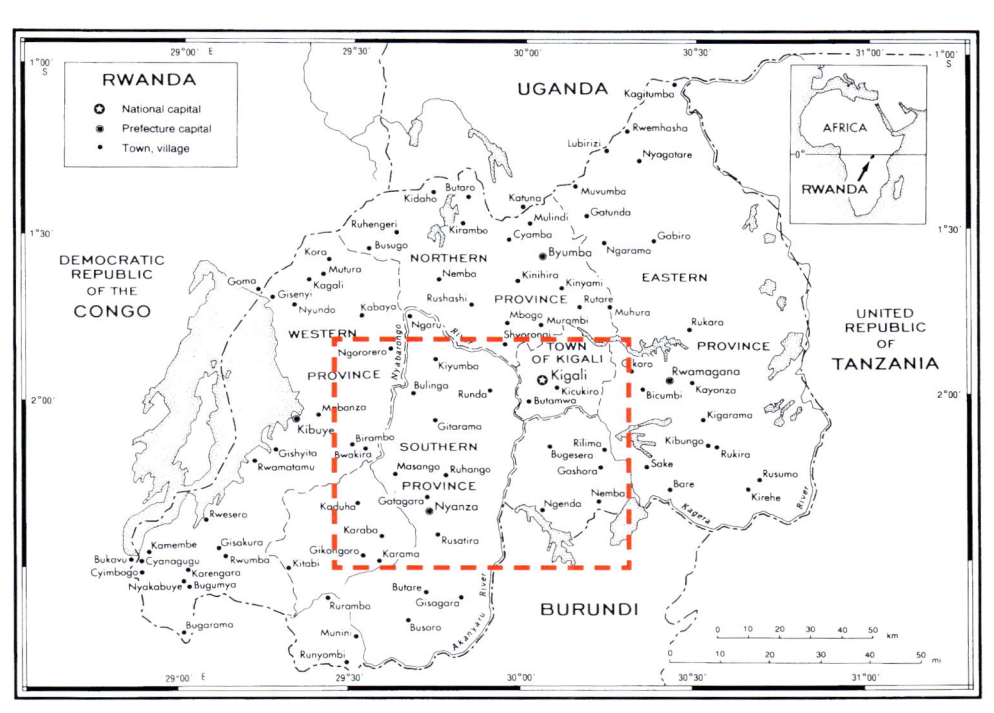

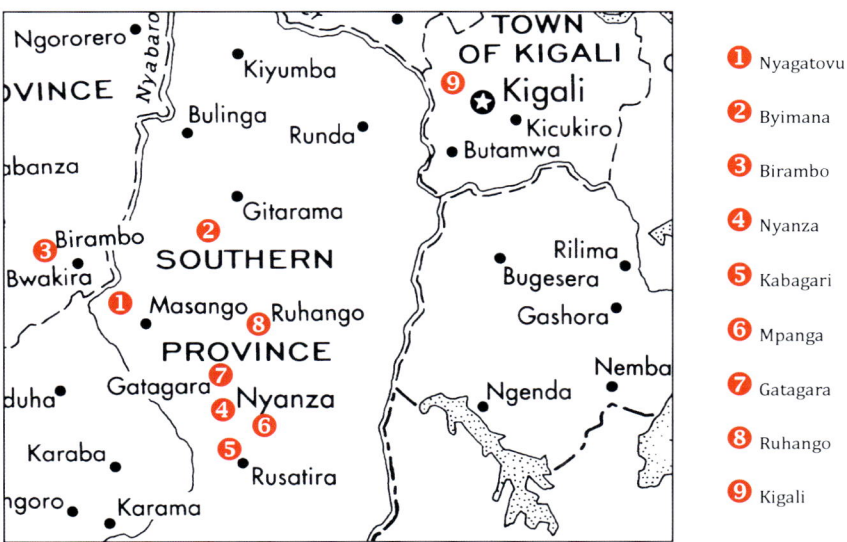

1. Nyagatovu
2. Byimana
3. Birambo
4. Nyanza
5. Kabagari
6. Mpanga
7. Gatagara
8. Ruhango
9. Kigali

Map: The Men Who Killed Me (Douglas & McIntyre, 2009)

TABLE OF CONTENTS

1.	THE SUN	11
2.	ON THE WAY TO HELL	15
3.	WHY AM I WRITING THIS BOOK?	21
4.	MY YOUTH	25
5.	THOSE WHO DO GOOD…	35
6.	THE RIOTS OF 1973	37
7.	A NEW PRESIDENT IN POWER	45
8.	THE INTELLECTUAL GENOCIDE	49
9.	THE BIRTH OF MY CHILDREN	55
10.	THE FIRST DAYS OF THE GENOCIDE	63
11.	ON THE RUN	73
12.	ISAAC AND HIS PREDICTION	77
13.	WILL IT NEVER STOP!	83
14.	THE BLACKEST DAY	95
15.	SAVED BY THE BIBLE	105
16.	HIDING AT OUR GODSON'S	111
17.	LONGING FOR DEATH	121
18.	THE RPF APPROACHES	127
19.	IN SEARCH OF HAPPINESS LOST	133
20.	THE FIRST CONTACT WITH SOLACE MINISTRIES	145
21.	MY LOST CHILDREN	157
22.	FORGIVE IN ORDER TO HEAL	169
23.	WITNESS FOR THE GACACA	185
24.	MY LIFE AND WORK AS A TRAUMA COUNSELLOR	197
25.	THE POWER OF RECONCILIATION	215
GLOSSARY		233
ACKNOWLEDGEMENTS		239
ABOUT THE AUTHORS		243
SOLACE MINISTRIES		245

THE SUN

The sun came up slowly, very slowly. Fumbling through the still perfect darkness, her light spun a gossamer thread on the horizon. Cautiously, the awakening dawn sought its way in the silent dark night. Weak rays carefully attempted to penetrate a world still cloaked in black, as if afraid of losing that newly-spun light. Their precocious glimmer created a decor of hazy, dark silhouettes.
Not for long though, because soon, flaring up on the horizon, a torrent of countless rays merged into a fiery beam and shot across the earth at a radiant, lightening speed. Unstoppable, the rays skimmed effortlessly past and over everything that they came into contact with, leaving behind them a trail of red.
They reigned for a moment over the land, the first messengers of a brand new day.
But then the sun appeared in all her majesty, throwing off her red cloak and allowing the ascending light to flood the land triumphantly and with complete devotion. A mighty halo of light gave chase to the last dark spectres and shadows.
Beneath the awakening sky, in the emergent light, unfolded a beautiful resplendent panorama, a paradise of green hills, fanning out from east to west, from north to south, flowing harmoniously into each other. Roads adorned the hills like red ribbons while rivers like polished silver flowed through valleys to the dark depths of cool lakes.
Rising and falling, the green rolled across the land and covered the hillsides in all shades imaginable. The hillsides coloured

themselves with the fresh green of coffee and tea bushes, the dark green of forests, the faded green of wild plants or with the soft green of banana plantations. The gleaming green of the rice fields sprawled out in the valley, marked by glistening waterways and sparkling fish ponds.

Under the illuminating eye of the rising sun the hills also appeared now, adorned with fields and meadows. Interwoven with each other in square patterns of green and red, they covered the outstretched hillsides like colourful rugs.

On the fertile ground grew beans, peas, carrots, potatoes, cassava, sorghum and many other nutritious plants. Each one defined its field with its own shade of green, sharply contrasting with the red of the earth. Red and green joined forces and, like a broad staircase, climbed the hill in terraces.

Spread out over the hillsides stood small huts with gardens. The early rays of the sun reflected off the thin metal of the corrugated iron roofs.

Narrow sand paths ran straight upwards or twisted, faint red and dusty, in feeble bends through the low grass, seeking their way past fields and bushes, leading to the red or clay huts on either side, losing their way in banana plantations or in the dense green around well-concealed farms.

Eucalyptus trees with their lofty narrow trunks and high broad canopies formed long avenues. Other trees seemed to have planted themselves randomly on the hillside or shared their green colours with each other and gathered in dense thickets.

Along with the dark of night the silence also fled. A dog barked angrily at the emerging day. The hoarse call of a crane echoed. Smoke circled reluctantly upwards from behind a hut. Voices could be heard as people emerged outside to greet the new day. The echo of a cheerful child's voice rolled down the hill.

Goats bleated, a cow lowed. Birds twittered loudly. All these sounds of the morning drifted down the hillside, cutting through the quickly evaporating tranquility.

On sandy pathways, past cassava and corn fields, sorghum and banana trees, there came a slow procession of people on their way to fetch water.

A woman in colourful clothing and headscarf walked elegantly and with careful steps, graceful in spite of the heavy burden she carried on her head. On the upward road a bicycle loaded with bananas slowly made its way uphill. A van passed by quickly. More and more people filled the roads, all starting the new day.

The town that had, more and more, caged her heart on the hilltop in rising concrete and glistening glass, stretched her broad asphalt arms out deep into the countryside. In the ascending light of the sun, the town awoke from the drowsiness of sleep and before long her streets filled with the noisy movement of people and the blaring sounds of cars and motors.

The sun had now sown the entire land with her light. An amazing land, the beautiful backdrop for a life of peace and happiness. A land whose people greeted the sun every morning with joy, to live and work in her light and warmth.

That's why the sun returned every morning. And she was back there again today.

The new day could begin.

"GOOD MORNING... RWANDA!"

ON THE WAY TO HELL

Shouting in the distance. Hard, raw voices; the pounding, rhythmic chanting of unintelligible slogans, hateful texts. Oh, I know them! The high, shrill sound of whistles from above, answered by short blasts from the other side, further along. There are a lot of them.

Rudely awoken from my sleep, my heart jumps and starts beating like crazy. The nails of my little boy, who I've already quickly strapped to my back as a precaution, claw frantically into the skin of my back through my clothing. Lambert is giving me a clear sign!

I push myself up carefully and my eyes search, staring in the potential direction of the threat.

In the shadow of a grove, covered by leaves and hidden behind branches, I try to get a look at my pursuers. I can't see for all the green so I push the branches to the side. Careful, not too loud! Keep calm!

For weeks already I've been on the run with my child strapped to my back. He has just turned one, but already carries inside him a human lifetime of fear and violence.

I prick up my ears; my eyes are searching again: still nothing, no one. In the forest where I've been hiding for a week and which has provided me with safety and shelter, I've made a bed of leaves. We were both able to restore our breath and get some air here in the last few days.

Before ending up here, I had already narrowly escaped my ruthless and merciless pursuers several times. As vigilant as prey for the hunter, alert to every suspicious sound, every unexpected movement, I lie here on the ground, ever alert, in fear of danger. Vigilance and caution have become second nature to me. I feel dejected.

Where are they now? I hear them going at it as if possessed. God, let them pass by and not find me! Go away!

Death has been stalking me for weeks. I've totally lost all sense of day and time. Only the transition of light and dark offers any kind of stability in my pitiful life. How long will we be safe here? Entire gangs parade early every day through the region. With their sharp machetes menacing in the air, glistening in the sun, rhythmically marching onwards, constantly singing the same rhymes, the same obscene chants. "Tuzabatsembatsemba!": "We are going to exterminate them!" Their humiliating, crude insults make crystal clear that they consider the Tutsis the lowest of the low. They have murderous intentions. They brandish any weapons that they can use to kill. Sticks, clubs, bats with nails and especially sharp machetes. Every now and then militia or men with rifles join the group. They work each other up, drink beer and turn into indiscriminate murderers. You do not want to fall into their hands!

Quiet! Quiet! The shouting and screaming is coming in my direction. I hear them now off to the side. Tense, my ears listen to the invisible noise in the unknown distance.

My human reasoning comes into acute conflict with my animal instinct. Which is the choice that will save my life? Staying here? Making a run for it? What other options do I have?

"Lambert, please don't make a sound. Even the slightest noise could give us away now!" But small though my youngest is, he senses unmistakably that making noise could bring danger.

Up until now my strong survival instinct has helped me to stay one step ahead of the pursuers. But I feel paralysing fear and panic rising inside me now, feelings which stifle me to such a degree that I lack the strength to keep running. Images of my children appear before me. I wonder how they are getting on. Are they still alive? And my brave husband, Placide? He sent me on the run with my youngest child. I shouldn't worry myself, he said. He and the other children would be fine. "You go and find somewhere safe."

Yes, I have to make it too. I have to go on, for their sakes. I will see them again! No, those murderers will not get me!

Oh, that noise, that racket, that whistling, it just goes on and on. I occasionally hear shrieking cheers. Another victim discovered, probably. The shouting swells to a roar. Fragments of words that I don't completely understand hang in the air a short distance from me.

A bang! A shot? Do I hear a rifle? Or is it an echo from the surrounding hills? I don't know anymore. All manner of thoughts rush through my mind. More roars of excitement from close by. Poor victims. They have my sympathy. The fugitives are no match for this feral mob, who drive them out from their hiding places like easy prey. You don't stand a chance against this pack of animals, wild, uncontrollable predators, prepared to horrifically slay anyone without pity in their triumphant frenzy. If they get their hands on you, you're lucky if it's a bullet that ends your life, because that is the most humane way to die. Anything is better than having these beasts hack off your limbs and leave you to die an unbearably painful death. Barbarians!

Quiet! They're getting close now. On all sides authoritative voices, the thrashing of machetes hacking a path through the forest. I hear branches creaking and breaking, the loud rustling noise of leaves sent flying into the air. They are really close now, somewhere behind me, indomitably fanatical behind their indomitably fanatical machetes. They talk, laugh with each other, breathing excitedly.

The blood rushes through my body, my thoughts are racing. Do not move an inch! I press myself closer against the ground, burying myself under the leaves.

I realise that the end is nigh. It's over for us. I've managed to keep myself hidden for so long, daring to cherish the hope of escaping all the violence.

Dark shadows are coming at me, striking and calling out to me.

I want to crawl deep into the ground. I hope for a miracle. They have walked by even more closely than this before. I don't fall for their lies! I have seen people give away their own hiding places when those bastards shouted: "Yes, we've seen you, you dirty snake. Come on out!"

My body trembles. There's no way out of this, I fear.

"Little Lambert, have all our efforts been in vain?"

Isaac then suddenly comes to my mind. Isaac who prayed for me and, yes, predicted that I would survive this violence and that he would see me and my child alive again!

Don't panic! Don't panic! Keep thinking! That is what has saved me up to now.

Then a loud creaking. Branches hit me in the face. A dark figure emerges suddenly from the shadows and yells out with triumphant contempt: "Here, here... two more! Come on out! Stand up! Quickly, filthy cockroaches! Hurry up!" He blows on his whistle. He hits me with his stick. A few of his companions come walking up: "Hey, another snake?" and someone strikes me on the legs. Lambert gets a slap as well. My body convulses. I struggle to stand up, scared, desperate. It is over. I get another smack. "Come on, you!" and pushing us in front of him, he leads us out of the forest to a wider road. On the way he rages: "Don't think about trying to trick us. Don't think we'll allow you the chance to get away! We will get all of you. All you slippery snakes and filthy cockroaches, we'll kill you all! Who else is there with you?" More beating. I try to resist. I try to comfort my child.

On the edge of the dirt track I see more prisoners; some are bleeding. A few Hutu men, many quite young, stand around, enflamed by the thrill of the hunt. One has blood on his hands and on his machete. He stamps on me. On my head. A young member of the Interahamwe militia hits me on my hand with his stick: "Your card! Show me your card!" They want my identity card which will indicate the ethnic group I belong to. A few simple deletions now determine my fate: life or death. But I already lost that card to them at a blockade. They took it away! I explain that my card was confiscated by their colleagues at a roadblock.

"You're a Tutsi and you don't want to admit it, you lying bitch." Another slap. "Stand there!" and he pushes me in the direction of those who share my destiny.

The pack of killers grows but also the number of prisoners. I see people vomiting, hear men, women begging for mercy, children crying, appealing to their father or mother for comfort, sobbing, eyes wide with fear. Some of them panic, they run away screaming and are brought forcefully back to the desperate group. Even the smallest get a slap. At that moment my children come once again to my mind.

Devils they are, disguised as people. They randomly hit out at everyone for no reason. Only to frighten us, to make us scared. They swear, call us every name under the sun just to humiliate us, to belittle us.

Fanatical youths, probably already drunk, together with the rest of their gang, form a tight circle and enclose us so that no one can get away. Lambert is quiet again.

From behind comes the order to start walking. A pathetic wailing procession staggers along the path and out of the forest. Marching to the rhythm of their dirty songs, full of hatred and contempt, the coldblooded murderers accompany us. We leave the forest and come to a wider road, direction Gatagara. Arriving in the village after a long walk, we are greeted to the left and right by the black burnt out remains of houses. Once the homes of innocent people, now dark carcasses, with dark empty doorways. They are the pathetic remnants of where people once lived in happiness. They serve as a warning of the fate that awaits us.

Our procession moves slowly onwards, in a kind of death march, to the centre, where other unfortunates have already been assembled and where Tutsi prisoners come down from several sides in rows, surrounded by the fanatical guards.

The villagers call after us as we walk past, spitting at us. Children laugh at us, swear or even hit us.

We are made to walk into the middle of the field. There, waiting for us, lies a wide freshly-dug shallow pit.

WHY AM I WRITING THIS BOOK?

If I'm going to describe my life and everything that's happened, I wonder in all seriousness if it's worth beginning with my youth. Is there any point looking back on events that belong to a long lost time? What value is there in stirring up memories of times destroyed in the dark red of the massacre that came crashing over me and many others?

If I dare summon up the courage to look back over my fate, in the distance I can make out the ghosts of my past and the surreality of a joyful and blessed existence in a world that has long since perished.

Through my tears I see a child that grew up in a harmonious family, I see the teacher who loved her profession and her pupils with heart and soul, I see the happy wife and mother of a big and beautiful family.

Her name is Beata, Beata Mukarubuga. She grew up to be an accomplished woman full of expectations and dreams for herself, her family and for many others, but whose day-to-day happiness, ideals and hopes for the future were horribly shattered by an unimaginably brutal violence.

Beata Mukarubuga. That's who I once was! Death ruthlessly seized power, carved the deepest wounds in me and alienated me from what I had once experienced as happiness.

My current desires no longer have their roots in my youth, in innocent thoughts, or in my beloved family.

My illusions have been brutally smashed to smithereens by the horrific things that people have done to each other.

The world of my youth has been destroyed at its very core. In the place where I lived for twenty-eight years nothing remains of what my family had built up over generations. All tangible memories have been wiped from the face of the earth. They themselves were all slaughtered, crushed, extirpated by the ruthless killing machine that was unleashed.

More than sixty years I've been living on this earth now. Fate, coincidence, God or whatever you want to call it, decreed I should be born in Rwanda. As a Tutsi, violence and bloodshed were already mine at birth. So many people are born in peace, so many die in peace. I, however, watched as peace was violated, hacked into pieces and left to bleed to death. I saw the sun set in the darkest, darkest black.

My dreams deteriorated into nightmares; the variegation of my country knew nothing but the deep, deep red that flowed from hundreds of thousands of mutilated bodies onto Rwandan soil. Soil drenched in blood. Blood mixed every day with the many tears of intense sorrow.

What does life still have to offer if the embodiment of everything that represents love is smothered by violence? Suddenly surrounded by monsters that want to kill you in the most barbaric way. Can I still speak of humanity here? I can't reconcile this in any way with the image of humanity that my contemporaries and I grew up with.

Who could I trust now? Who could I depend on? Those who I had previously greeted warmly, treated with respect and offered a helping hand to, turned against me with contempt and crude violence.

Future? Was there still a future for me?

What kind of a life lied ahead for me? Yes, my heart beat, I breathed, my eyes saw and my ears heard. My body was alive. But aimless and pointless? I no longer recognised the life that I once sought, once found.

My despair pushed a dismal thought to the surface: did I actually want to continue this grey existence? I longed for an end to all my dejection and misery.

However, I am still alive. Deep within me there was still a glimmer of hope, a little courage, to accept my new future with a heavy heart, and not shut myself away and let myself sink away into mourning for my destroyed past.

In spite of the intense sorrow and the terrible pain, I saw a chance to accept life again and to give it meaning.

For God, who supported me in such a remarkable way that He managed to convince me of His miraculous powers. Thanks to His help I survived the genocide; thanks to His help I survived mourning and melancholy. Together with me He sought a way towards a new and acceptable life. He stood by me when I needed to struggle through the greatest troubles and obstacles. I promised to bear witness to His greatness.

For my three children who survived the slaughter, by taking responsibility for their upbringing.

For my fellow man, by putting myself at their service and standing by them.

I was well aware that building a new life without my husband and five of my children would be very rough and it would require a lot of time, patience, effort and persistence. But I found a way and accepted the challenge. For years I have walked that road, the roughest road of my life, with its ups and downs, with tears and comfort, but I have never given up.

I turned my back on death and led myself back to life. To this I bear witness. I make you the spectator of the most horrific period of my life. So many others had to go through what I endured. Many, very many people, from family to colleagues, from friends to fellow villagers, did not survive the horrors. I did.

Should I be happy that I'm still alive? Now I can say: Yes. Yes, I am thankful that I am still alive. Just as the sun rises from the black night and slowly spreads its light across the earth, so must I rise now from a black void and let the light shine once again into my life. Not until years and years after the genocide, did I feel able, without becoming defiant, to recognise the fundamental value of forgiveness and reconciliation in my life, and I discovered the therapeutic qualities of both. Both offered me, with my physically and mentally damaged body, perspective to believe in the future. I'm telling my life story to offer comfort to people and to tell them why I chose life.

Tears flow, but you don't see them. I know pain and sorrow. I feel the intense loss of so many dear and precious people. Still I say: I will go on!

I found myself in the fortunate position of coming into contact with people who convinced me to believe in life again. They did that in such a warm and inspiring way that the need to help the survivors of the genocide grew within me.

Helping them by giving them courage and self-confidence, but more importantly by nurturing a sense of self-worth and playing a part in the healing of the deep wounds left by the genocide. I want to tend their deeply painful scars, ease their suffering and offer them hope for the future. Partly by way of my life story.

In this story, however, I want to bear witness to a world in which discrimination and prejudice led to deadly hatred and violence, and to offer a warning against the awful consequences that followed. I offer this warning because there are still people on this earth who do not consider all humans to be equals, who mistrust and despise each other, and as long as this state of affairs persists there remains the possibility of future violent conflicts.

I christen my pen in tears and write a story that actually cannot be captured in words, because for three months I lived in close quarters with feelings of fear and tension and mainly with death. I describe the life of Beata Mukarubuga.

This name is, however, a memory. The name Beata belongs to a world soaked in so much blood, to a life in which her happiness was crushed and she lost her husband and five children.

The deeply tragic consequences of the genocide forced me to build a new life for myself. The name Beata no longer fits with this new life though. From now on call me Mama Lambert. As Mama Lambert I also christen my pen in hope and write about my life after the genocide. A story about my new future.

MY YOUTH

My parents gave me the name Beata. Beata means 'bringing luck'. I was their first child.

I was born in Rwanda on December 28th 1952 in Nyagatovu, a small village located on a small hill. Nyagatovu belonged to the Masango commune in the prefecture of Gitarama. So my name is Beata Mukarubuga, daughter of Eliezer Gakwaya, my father, and Maria Mukakimenyi, my mother. In Rwanda being the eldest child means fulfilling an important role in the family. Parents project their expectations onto the eldest child and that brings additional responsibilities for that child... for me then.

After me came two other children: my brother Elias Munyarubuga and my sister Rosalie Mukankubito.

Our family also grew in an unexpected way, although not uncommon in Rwanda: a sister of my father was not capable of providing the necessary care for her five children and so my father took it upon himself to provide that care. We welcomed our little cousins into our family and after time we were so used to the situation that we considered them our natural brothers and sisters. Only on the day they got married, they left our house to live elsewhere. Sadly, they were all killed during the genocide. Our village numbered around fifty families and their houses were spread out over the hill. We lived right at the top and within our ample grounds were several buildings, a few of which functioned as a furnished family home. We looked out over the many hills that surrounded us and a little further along in the valley flowed the Masango river.

My family had lived in Nyagatovu for generations and, among others, grandpa and grandma, uncles and aunts lived close by, as did at least five of my father's brothers. If we wanted to visit his three sisters then we had to go a little further afield because they all lived a considerable distance away. My mother's two sisters and four brothers didn't live too far away either.

My future husband, Placide, lived there too and his parents, Jean Baptiste Gafaranga and Annonciata Mutumwinka, were good friends with mine.

Whenever there was something to celebrate we all made our way over there and all the old stories were told. And I can still hear my grandparents saying "... never to live without cows", because cows represented prosperity and well-being. Grandpa and grandma also impressed upon us the importance of thanking God in prayer, of saying grace before eating, and of praying after getting up in the morning and before retiring at night.

Not far from our house was the parish church where a white priest was in service. I thought the priest was very nice. He didn't just provide religious instruction, he also surprised us now and then with bread rolls. For me that was a real treat because you couldn't buy anything so tasty in our village. The people had a lot of respect for the priest because he was an honourable man. If the priest came calling, that was reason enough for my father to make clear to us that, inside or outside the house, we should play quietly and not scream or shout.

On Sunday we went to mass with our parents and that meant a lot of work the Saturday before. Our parents tasked us with cleaning the church and setting out the seats.

On Sunday morning we walked to church to celebrate with the other villagers, and during the service to pray and to sing. We often sang Latin hymns, which I can still remember now. After Mass there was no work. We visited neighbours or relatives and played with friends or cousins.

Next to the church there was a small centre for spiritual education, including catechism classes and preparation for religious celebrations and ceremonies. The priest of our parish supervised the running of the school strictly and, when he deemed it necessary, he disciplined the teachers who taught us. My primary school consisted of six school years. I remember that sometimes there were as many as fifty-five pupils in a class. Lessons began at eight o'clock in the morning and continued until twelve o'clock. We rounded off the morning by saying our Hail Marys and we went home to eat. Children who lived further away brought food with them and came to our house to ask for water, but they actually meant banana juice. My mother knew exactly what it was they wanted. She put the cups on the table, filled them with banana juice and gave it to them to drink. We had to make sure we were back at school again by one o'clock. When the schoolday was over at four o'clock, we walked home again either to play or to help on the farm.

We had a farm with many cows and quite a few fields; we grew potatoes, beans, peas, carrots and cassava there. Fruit trees provided us with many types of fruit and we grew bananas in a plantation. The climate in Rwanda is perfect for growing produce the whole year round. My parents allowed the church to use a piece of land to grow vegetables. And then there were also the fields where the cows grazed. There were neighbours who didn't have any cows but who did have land. Our cows were allowed to graze on that land in exchange for milk. Or my father paid the people for the use of their land. We also owned a small forest where we gathered wood so that we could cook.

We children also helped on the farm; we fed the chickens, we fed the calves, we picked vegetables and also fetched water from a stream.

During the rain season we became completely wet during those chores because of the many showers. That's why we made rain screens of banana leaves and held these above our heads to stay dry.

Rwanda is home to many rivers, and at the bottom of our hill flowed the Masango river.

Fetching water was a job for girls. For water we had to walk quite a distance and so took us a fair amount of time. With a stone urn or pot on our heads we went down the hill, drew water from a stream that flowed into the Masango and with a fairly heavy urn made our way back up the hill.

If my mother made banana juice, she needed a lot of water and we had to make many trips down the hill and back up again to fetch litres and litres of water, which cost us an extra lot of time and effort.

I enjoyed helping my parents. Girls also helped around the house with the cleaning and the preparation of food. The older boys busied themselves with the more physical work. The younger boys took the cows off to graze.

We also helped mum to make wicker mats. With other girls we sang songs as we gathered reeds by the river. I also played with friends who lived close by. We played ball games or one of the many chase-and-catch games that we knew, or we played hide-and-seek.

Our relationship with the other neighbours on the hill was good and we considered each other friends. In our village Hutus, Tutsis and Twas lived side by side in harmony. For generations peace had prevailed and there was a strong sense of trust, which enabled us to form a close village community. We had a lot of time for each other. There were several communal activities organised in the village. People were prepared to help each other, certainly in the event of illness or ill-fortune. We felt as though we were one family. You could just walk into people's homes. If you happened to be at someone's house and dinner was ready, you sat yourself down on the floor and you ate with them. If there was juice, then you drank juice.

Families brought up children from other families and that was considered normal. It was also fairly common to ask one of the neighbours to be godparent to your child.

Poorer people who were having a hard time came by to see if they could help out or maybe come and work. There was often work to be done and my father rewarded their work with vegetables and fruit from our fields.

These days it's unthinkable, but when I was a child people didn't have radio or television. There was no telephone either. I've already mentioned that the sense of community was very strong and that families brought up each other's children. Within our family we also had a lot of contact with each other and we saw uncles and aunts regularly. When we went to fetch water, during the harvest or vacation, for example, we played with their children, our cousins.

Through the years, with the advent of modern media, that sense of community and the family bond have been weakened considerably. These same media now bring us speedily up to date with what is going on in the world.

If during my youth there was ever any news to report, then it was delivered by a messenger. It wasn't unusual to give someone a message to deliver if they were leaving the village. These messengers often travelled by foot.

I remember that the missionary had a horse that he rode around on and there were also already people in the village who had cars. One or two even had a radio.

How were we kept informed about (political) developments in our country or region, or plans or decisions made in the municipality? How did we get to know what the government, the prefect or the mayor wanted us to know?

The prefect was the person in charge over all communes in the prefecture. He was senior to the mayors, or 'bourgmestres', who led the municipalities together with the village councils, known as the 'conseils'. The conseil consisted of important people who lived in the municipality. When there was important information to announce to the villagers of our village, that news came in through the 'centre de conseil', the community centre and, for special occasions or important decisions, all residents received an invitation to gather there.

In 1959 I turned seven years old. A child that lived under a lucky star and in a safe, sheltered world of everyday certainties. Through my innocence I remained ignorant of the tensions around me, tensions that were growing between the groups that called themselves Hutus and Tutsis. I was a child who had no idea what was about to happen in our country.

Although, that same year I did notice a change in the atmosphere which did nothing to promote mutual trust. When certain people saw my father, they started to whisper to each other or broke off their conversations. Some neighbours stopped greeting us. Here and there houses burned down.

From conversations I understood that there was a chance it could all go wrong at any moment. Good relations were strained, life was no longer humming along as it should. Various neighbours got together to discuss the situation.

That's when I began to notice the signs of what would many years later result in violent massacre. One day, a well-meaning neighbour came to warn us that some of the other neighbours were planning to kill all the Tutsis on the hill, after which all their cows would be taken. As a precaution, father sent us women and children to grandma and the men fled into the forest.

I slept with grandma, but was startled awake one night by men shouting, the high shrill sound of whistles and the lowing of the cows. It was a terrible noise. I jumped out of bed. Everyone was incredibly shaken and waited anxiously to see what would happen.

The attackers threw stones on the roof and at the cows, who ran off in all directions at random, lowing. What should I do? Any moment, those bad men would break in and beat me. I hid behind a large pile of wicker mats where sorghum and beans were normally kept, anxiously clamping my hands over my eyes, and waited to see if they would discover me. Only my toes were sticking out.

"Where is Gakwaya?" screamed Nyilinkwaya, one of our neighbours, referring to my father. "I'm going to hack off his head," he said, as he kicked violently against the door. Grandma opened the door and asked:

"Friend, why do you want to kill us?"

"What did you say, bitch? Must I beat you to death?"

I heard his companions call her various names as they hit her and threatened to kill her. Grandma begged Nyilinkwaya to spare us all. "What! Those little snakes, I have no sympathy for them," he screamed and he raised his stick and beat grandma severely all over her body until she groaned with pain. For the rest of her days she lived with the pain of that beating.

I heard other men shout: "Come on now! This is taking far too long! Hurry up! We'll go and get the cows first!"

Rukebesha, another neighbour, wanted to set fire to the house. This same Rukebesha would later play a significant role in the planning and execution of the killings.

Grandma quickly gathered her grandchildren together and we all fled. We moved to the home of my father's youngest brother and on the way there we saw many Tutsi houses on fire, the arsonists having already taken any possessions beforehand.

On the second night, we saw father again and he led us to some bushes to hide ourselves in nearby caves and pits. Every day we moved from one hiding place to another.

Many Tutsis no longer felt safe due to the multitude of violent disturbances, threats, looting and vandalism, and they fled across the border. Two of my mother's brothers sought refuge in Uganda during those disturbances. My father, however, wanted to remain in our village despite the destruction of our house and the physical assault that grandma suffered, which left her unable to walk.

'Muyaga' is a wind and nobody knows where it comes from. It comes without warning and just as suddenly is gone again.

After two weeks the riots were over. The members of the conseil, agitators and co-instigators of the riots, which had led to murder and looting, now called on all Hutus to put an end to the violence. To us Tutsis they said: "Come back! We are sorry for everything that's happened. Let's start over again. Life goes on!"

Not all Hutus showed remorse for what they had done. Far from it. Others, however, helped us to rebuild our house and brought back the stolen tiles from the destroyed houses. We fetched wood from the forest, renovated the house and also mended the enclosure for the cows. The cows had been slaughtered and the meat taken away by the perpetrators. We'd only found the remains the following day in the meadow. We bought new cows when the rebuilding work was completed.

Tutsis who had also gone on the run and who had gone into hiding also returned to their houses to repair them.

Life carried on, but I had lost the innocence of being a child. My safe world had imploded after the terrible events that had happened to me and my family. Some of the kind neighbours that we'd always gotten on so well with had threatened us and looted our property just like that!

I was really shaken up. Unexpected noises brought back the fear. If a branch broke off in the forest, my heart started beating twice as fast.

Only years later I realised that the Hutus' hatred of the Tutsis was systematically fueled and it ultimately resulted in horrific atrocities. During the Belgian mandate in Rwanda, the mistrust between the Hutu and Tutsi populations was already on the rise and during the run-up to the declaration of independence in 1962, both parties tried to make themselves as strong as possible in order to gain the best possible position in the new independent government.

The violent outbreaks of 1959 were caused by the fact that the Tutsi king Mwami had died in suspicious circumstances. And when an attack on the Hutu leader Grégoire Kayibanda of the MDR Parmehutu was foiled, Rwanda entered a spiral of ever-increasing violence. In the same year that I celebrated my seventh birthday, ten thousand Tutsis were murdered and tens of thousands more fled for their lives to neighbouring Uganda, where they lived in exile and waited until the time was right to return safely to Rwanda.

The years after 1959 were relatively calm and life went back to normal.

My parents, concerned about me, advised me: "Look ahead, not back! Be courageous and take your studies seriously to build a good future for yourself."

On July 1st 1962 - I was nine at the time - we held a big party in our village to celebrate the proclamation of the independence of Rwanda. The Belgians had withdrawn from our country and from Burundi. We now had an independent government with a Rwandan president in charge. The first president was called Grégoire Kayibanda, a Hutu, who was also the leader of the MDR Parmehutu, the only party in the political arena.

The following year rumours were rife that the Tutsis - the 'inyenzi' or 'cockroaches' - who lived abroad wanted to return to Rwanda. That was legally forbidden by the government, because they were afraid that these Tutsis would form an army and seize power.

For one whole week there were also disturbances near us. Riots broke out, people were murdered, fires were started. There were bodies floating in the Nyabarongo river, I heard. The members of the conseil swiftly intervened to prevent the violence from spreading. With the exception of the looting of several fields, our Hutu neighbours kept calm and there were no incidents worth mentioning on our hill. Calm slowly returned and in the years that followed we remained safe from new incidents.

It's remarkable that neither the government nor the local leaders announced sanctions against the murderers and looters. No one was ever arrested or prosecuted.

I sometimes wonder: Why did we Tutsis put up with all that murder and destruction without protest? The atmosphere became so tense at times that any unacceptable behaviour of one Tutsi, anywhere in the land, provoked the anger of a crowd of Hutus. Riots then erupted everywhere and they vented their anger on us with beatings and looting as a consequence.

In 1964 I began the last year of primary school. I sat the national entrance examination for high school, which I passed with excellent grades. After primary school I was admitted to secondary education on the recommendation of our parish priest. That was unusual because the government had regulated admission to secondary education by law so that you were selected predominantly on grounds of ethnicity rather than merit. Hutus, a large majority in Rwanda, had a huge advantage when it came to admission to secondary education. As a Tutsi my chances were minimal. Thanks to the intervention of our village's white priest, I managed to get a high school education. I was now being educated at Byimana, a high school that was run by a congregation of Catholic nuns.

My childhood was now behind me.

THOSE WHO DO GOOD…

Small, seemingly unimportant things sometimes have a greater effect than you could ever imagine. The way I see it, I am able to write this book about my life due to a small gesture I made as a teacher to a student.

After attending the Catholic missionary primary school and three years of high school, my prospects of further study in Byimana were limited. One of the few courses open to Tutsis was the teacher training programme. That school was in Birambo and I applied, as so many Tutsis did, because of the restrictions. My studies lasted two years and I earned my teaching diploma in July 1970.

I began my career at the Nyagatovu primary school. Despite being more or less forced by circumstances into teacher training, I found myself really enjoying my work as a teacher. My teaching style was highly valued and I taught for twenty-four years up until 1994. I taught children in their last year of primary school and prepared them for the national entrance exam for high school education.

I loved teaching. Teaching is a profession, but I definitely saw it as a calling. I defined this by dedicating myself with heart and soul to my pupils and guiding these children with the necessary attention in their growth towards adulthood.

Every year we teachers were assessed. As a teacher I was highly thought of because my classes stood out due to their high quality.

I was praised for my abilities, dedication and management and therefore always scored well in the assessment.

My pupils all came from different backgrounds: Hutu children, Tutsi children and Twa children. The children of rich parents, the children of poor parents, it made no difference to me, they were all equally dear to me. I still feel grateful when former pupils come and visit me out of appreciation for what I was able to do for them and I see it as acknowledgement of the work and the time that I devoted to them.

I paid special attention to the children whose parents weren't able to get hold of school materials. I was able to help these pupils by letting them use school materials or even my own pen so that they could write and they had no reason to fall behind.

I remember the school year when I regularly lent my BIC-pen to one of the boys, a Twa. Munyaneza his name was. With that pen, he was able to do his exercises or jot down everything I had written up on the board.

Years later, during the genocide, I would find out that in the eyes of this child, my small gesture of lending him that BIC-pen had left a greater impression on him than I could have ever imagined.

THE RIOTS OF 1973

In 1973, I started my 21st year. It was the year I was to come of age, but turned out to be a year that would cast its shadow far into the future. In 1973, I - along with many other Tutsis - was confronted with a discriminating, even life-threatening intolerance.

I had worked for more than two years in primary education. I already had the required experience and would go as far as to say I was a serious and dependable teacher, so I received a permanent position that offered me a regular salary.

I still lived at home and considered myself fortunate, as our family was prosperous. Our cows not only provided milk, but also manure, which we spread over the fields. Beans, peas and a variety of other vegetables grew on the fertilised soil. We cultivated bananas on our plantation and in other fields we grew manioc, sorghum, coffee and all kinds of fruit trees.

Happiness and peace were also revived in our hearts.

On the morning of February 1st, however, my father woke with a start from a terrible nightmare. Still recovering from the shock, he stammered that he had witnessed an explosion of violence: many Tutsis had fled or died at the hands of murderers.

All our animals were slaughtered. What he remembered most vividly from his dream, he told us in his shaken state, was the woeful cries of children and fearful lowing of cows.

Mama responded angrily: "When will you get those somber thoughts and nasty dreams out of your head! You know that the culprits - all those who participated in the riots - have openly expressed regret for the misdeeds they committed in the past years. This will really never happen again! It's all in the past! Forget it, please!" Of course we desperately hoped that those terrible events would never be repeated, but we cherished that wish in vain.

Three days later, late in the evening, we heard screaming outside. There were ominous cries: "OO-oo-oo-oo...! OO-oo-oo-oo...! OO-oo-oo-oo...!!"

What was going on? What did all that noise mean? My father leapt up and immediately ran outside. Fleeting shadows shot away in the darkness, with much turmoil further on. Then his niece Gicari came running out of the darkness, crying. She had slept at grandmother's, but a mob of people had burst into the house, beaten her, and set the whole place on fire. The cows were also taken.

My father took Gicari inside in shock, but feared that his dream had been completely confirmed when a couple of minutes later his nephew Ntaganda, son of his youngest brother Michel, burst into our house out of breath. Gasping, he cried: "They plundered our house and set it on fire! I heard a group of screaming men arrive and quickly drove the cows to a safe place. I wanted to return home, but from far off I could already see the flames rising from the roof!"

He told us that his parents had both fled and he had come to warn us to seek refuge as quickly as possible.

"A gang of neighbours are after our possessions. A great deal has been taken from our house and those people destroyed lots of things. Everything is now on fire! Run! It won't be long before they get here. Make sure you get away!" After these words he disappeared as fast as he had come.

My father thought it was best for us to hide in the nearest woods. The terrifying cries of "OO-oo-oo-oo.. ! OO-oo-oo-oo...! OO-oo!" continued all night long. Many Tutsis fled their houses, ran for their lives and tried to save themselves by hastily seeking shelter in woods and undergrowth.

Papa insisted that we girls hide in a safe place. Women and

girls had to be particularly careful to avoid being raped. "Let's not reproach ourselves with anything. If death has to cross our paths, let's die as brave heroes. That will give a clear, powerful signal to those unjust and criminal people."

At that moment I became very frightened and felt an oppressive terror of death rising inside me. I ran away quickly to find shelter at the house of a Hutu girl, my godchild. We had such a good relationship with her family that we even paid for her studies and regularly gave the family part of our harvest.

I was permitted to stay the night, but the next morning they chased me away, because they had heard that my uncle, Michel Rwabuneza, was an agitator. That was completely untrue, but they saw it as a just reason to get rid of me.

My uncle Michel had done no one any harm. He got on well with everyone, but if he was treated discourteously, he was completely fearless in dealing with people. He summoned the courage to defend himself against Hutu attacks, even threatening revenge if they were to do anything to him: "Just you try setting my house on fire! If my house burns, so will yours! Keep your hands off my cows! You're Christians too! Don't you know the Ten Commandments? You know perfectly well what you can and can't do, you scoundrels!"

Thanks to that false tale about my uncle, my godchild's family threw me out just like that and I walked home, afraid.

But that was a disaster. At home I found everything destroyed and burnt. Only mama was walking around in despair; the others had fled. Mama herself had not been mistreated or threatened with death. One of the perpetrators had decided to spare her because she had regularly given him and his family milk and food. He even praised my mother in public, saying that she fed his children when they hungrily walked past our house after attending the parochial school.

When mama saw me fit and healthy, she burst into tears and thanked God for protecting me, like a hen watching over her chicks by hiding them under her wings. To protect me from all evil she hung a rosary around my neck.

After a while my 15-year old sister Rosalie ran up and warned us, panting, that the attackers would come back later. First the cursed people were planning to go to Gakwaya's house before proceeding to the homes of my father and Jean Munyaruyonga, a neighbour. After that it would be the turn of my uncles, Michel Rwabuneza, Gaspard Sebucaca and Stephan Mutayomba, then my father's aunt Veronique, and finally other neighbours who lived spread out on the hill.

My sister overheard these evil plans when she went looking for a hiding place in the banana plantation belonging to our neighbour Rukebesha. This Hutu neighbour would continue to play a significant role in the organised attacks on our family. During the genocide he largely achieved his aim. Now he is a trembling old man who cannot remember anything.

One morning we heard the shrill, piercing whistles and cries of noisy, murderous men. A disorderly hoard chased after my uncle Michel. They threw long spears at him which pierced the air with a whooshing sound and landed on the ground in precisely the spot he had just fled. They threatened to overcome him, but he bolted full speed into the house of Murema, a kind Hutu. Murema came out almost immediately swinging a spear and snarled at the group: "The hunt's over, because your quarry is in my house." The gang, trumped by Murema, withdrew and came to our house. By behaving so boldly, this Hutu saved my uncle Michel.

However, now all those men hurried over to our house. When they found no one there, they searched the place, discovered our tracks and made off after us with bellowing hunting cries, while we ran as fast as we could down the hill of Nyagatovu.

A little later we reached the river Masango and fled straight on through it. We ran up the hill of Rwoga, which was inhabited by Tutsis, a number of whom were married to Hutus. Because of the mixed marriages, no violent incidents had occurred there so far, though that would soon change during the genocide.

On the other side the old man Zirimaso, another good Hutu, happened to be grazing his cows and recognised his son and two grandsons in the group of pursuers. Bravely he took up position in the middle of the road and prevented our wild tormentors from pursuing us any longer. Indignantly, he shouted at the gang that they should respect the tradition which forbids Rwandans from chasing girls and women, exploding again with rage at the group and adding that women and girls were a very easy target. However, the agitated people were so carried away with it all that they did not even listen to Zirimaso, who began to curse them. Without taking any notice of the Hutu, they pushed him aside and the gang chased after us again, now on the other side of the hill.

At a house a little further on stood an old man we did not know, but with whom we sought refuge. He gestured to a small house next to his own, urging us to go in "quickly, quickly" as I heard him say that the enemy was already very close by. We hesitated. Was it a trap? If he was tricking us, it would not be difficult for our pursuers to catch us, but there was no time to think or to choose. Inside!

Fortunately the old man meant well. He even grabbed his bow and aimed an arrow at the gang, threatening them: "Where did you learn the custom that Rwandan men chase women, huh?" and he shot his arrow straight at the threatening gang, wounding one of them. The men now stopped, and slunk away, dragging the wounded man with them. We were saved.

The house that offered us protection turned out to be a goat shed and among the animals we were able to catch our breath. In thanks for our salvation we prayed to God, a prayer that my mother regularly prayed not only for us, but for all Tutsis.

During our attempt at escape someone who lived next door to old Joseph, one of our neighbours, had been killed in the village. Even my father had been in great danger, but he had managed to disguise himself so that he narrowly escaped the same fate. He had dressed himself as a woman, with a headscarf and a cloth around his legs to cover up his trousers. Dressed like this he fled to the hill on the other side, mainly inhabited by Tutsis descended from Basinga.

Mother did not stay at home to await the murderous gang but

also fled to Rwoga, without knowing our situation. She hid in the woods where everyone knew a leopard lived.

After a few days we heard gunshots again for the first time. They came from soldiers from the northwest region of Bakiga. We heard that a revolutionary upheaval had drastically changed political relationships in Rwanda. The new commander Habyarimana, who came from the region, had ordered the soldiers to restore peace. They stated that president Kayibanda was too weak and incompetent to rule the country, so they felt obliged to call a halt to the chaos and put things in order. They assured us that no more Tutsis would be killed!

Myself, after the attack of Hutus in 1973.

Paul Gahamanyi (left) and my husband Placide (right) talk about how they survived the attack of 1973.

A NEW PRESIDENT IN POWER

The serious riots that caused us to flee did not last long. They heralded a coup intended to overthrow president Kayibanda.

The revolution arose from a battle which had been running for some time, causing unrest between Hutu inhabitants from Nduga in the south and those from Rukiga in the north. This was really a case of regional segregation. Kayibanda, our first president, came from the south, and Habyarimana, the one in power after the coup, was a man from the north. The tensions between Hutus from the north and those from the south were partly due to the coup. When conflict threatened to break into violence between the two regions due to rising tensions, the Hutus all over the country spread false rumours so that Tutsis could be scapegoated for the dispute, and this often resulted in Tutsis becoming the victims.

Strangely enough, I do not remember the precise dates when the change of power took place. I was not aware of it. For too long we had had to hide in the daytime, and to try to find food or wash in the river at night. All the terrible events had disrupted the regularity of my life and my sense of the rhythm of the days had disappeared.

Due to the change in power, many Tutsis were able to return home, or rather to the places where their homes had stood. In many cases the houses lay in ruin, most of the cows had been slaughtered and many possessions plundered. Our only comfort was that we ourselves were still alive.

Slowly we picked up the thread of our lives again, along with the others who had escaped the massacres. The dead were buried, ruined houses rebuilt, work resumed. However, many Tutsis, mainly younger people, left for neighbouring countries such as Burundi, Congo, Uganda and Tanzania.

My father sought contact with the soldiers who were lodging in the school and responsible for safety in the region. He urged them to ask the Hutus who were guilty of the destruction of our possessions at least to help in the rebuilding of our houses. The soldiers listened to his request and encouraged Hutus to help with the renovation. What we did not ask of those Hutus was to bring back the cows they had taken. There was no point, as those animals, of course, were no more.

One of our houses was rebuilt, with the roof tiles that the Hutus returned. The first restored house had to accommodate six families, thirty-two people altogether. Due to lack of space the women and children slept inside and the men outside. For four months we had to live in primitive conditions, waiting for the restoration of the other destroyed houses. When our houses and those of the other families were ready, everyone was able to return to their own dwellings.

We made our house even bigger, which was possible with my salary and the profits from the coffee plantation. We even bought two cows, which reproduced wonderfully quickly and regularly bore calves.

Our faith in life was restored, reinforced by the promises of the new president Habyarimana. At the start of his term of office he made a promising speech. He expressed criticism for Hutus who had killed their neighbours, with whom they shared everything. These neighbours had always provided mutual support, been baptised at the same time, or forged a family relationship by entering into marriage. The president openly asked who had encouraged the violence, and who had instigated the vicious treatment of their neighbours.

Habyarimana wanted to come across as peace-loving to win over the population. He emphasised that Kayibanda had failed to stop the massacres. The new president also underlined the need for the coup:

"This coup was carried out to emphasise and maintain equality between all ethnic and social groups. In the past few years we have seen ethnic problems raise their head again. That's why we had to intervene, to advance the foundations of the revolution and to confirm the principle of equality between all groups within our population."

We followed his words at home through a transistor radio that my father had bought. Neighbours came by to listen with us and, gathered in suspense around the blue Philips receiver, together we heard the new president's speech.

The president furthermore explained in his speech that the MDR Parmehutu, Kayibanda's party, had been abolished and replaced by his own party, the MRND. From then on there was only one party in Rwanda, but that party was intended for all sectors of the population. He intended his party to be a boat crossing the sea of poverty, loaded with the best intentions to combat that poverty and leave it behind on the way to prosperity.

His motto was "Ubumwe, Amahoro, Amajyambere", or "Unity, Peace and Development". The president also sketched a new future for all inhabitants, in which peace would be the big winner. Peace for everyone, he promised.

His speech was very significant and strengthened our hope for better times. Elated, we applauded. We looked at one another cheerfully. What he said was almost unbelievable to us. Were the massacres, the slaughter, really a thing of the past? Would it be possible to live in harmony together?

Although there remained some doubt among us after all the previous attacks on Tutsis, the new president came across as a good person. He restored our belief in society; everyone was overjoyed about the new future. My parents also felt that we had acquired a good president.

The president became famous for his beautiful words. People wrote and sang about him, dancing in his honour; people wore clothing and medals with his image. He regularly addressed the people and his speeches were a joy to the ears. His words had to bring peace to the hearts of the people and dissipate the fear of violence. For that reason he was given the name 'Umubyeyi', which means 'Father of the people'. Wherever he went, young and old chanted his name: "Umubyeyi! Umubyeyi! Umubyeyi!"
I still remember his face from the photo that hung in our school.

THE INTELLECTUAL GENOCIDE

But what did seem strange to me (and still does) was that no one went to court, and just as with earlier violent incidents, none of the perpetrators were punished, nor were any of the victims compensated.

No, and the jobs many Tutsis had lost before 1973 because of a population quota were not given back to them either. On the contrary! The president's MRND party seemed more and more to reflect the Hutu point of view. Party members - Hutus - were rewarded with nice jobs like mayor, administrative officer, sub-prefect or other positions in the political party that now had power.

The president also maintained what I like to call the 'intellectual genocide': a discriminatory limit on admissions to secondary education for Tutsi students. That remained unchanged. Even more, Habyarimana made this limit law. He thereby confirmed the so-called ethnic quota in higher education. This system was drawn up based on the percentage of people belonging to each ethnic group. Of the people living in Rwanda 85% were Hutus, 10% were Tutsis and 5% were Twas.

For the education system, that meant that 85% Hutu primary school students could continue on to secondary school after passing the examination, and only 10% Tutsi students.

As a Tutsi I was held back in my own education by the government's ethnic quota. My chances of continuing my studies were minimal. There were six years of high school. I finished five years, but for Tutsis there was not much left to choose from after the third year. Teacher training was one of my few options for years four and five. But completing a sixth year that would have given me the right to go to the university, was barred to me because I was a Tutsi.

This unjust and senseless system was very painful to me, all the more so because now I taught the last year of primary school. I was powerless to change anything when a less talented Hutu child was favoured over a Tutsi child who clearly had more ability.

Tutsis were regarded as inferior. We were so used to being called words like 'inyenzi' (cockroach) and 'serpent' (snake) that they didn't seem unfamiliar to us anymore when we heard them. A Tutsi had been degraded to inhuman status, to a kind of animal. And what an animal! Yes, we accepted it! "Hey, you cockroach!" We just laughed along with them. If you objected, you ran the risk of getting a beating.

"Watch out for that serpent!" parents called to their children, feeding a climate of intolerance and degradation, of contempt and discrimination. "Kill that serpent!"

Referring to this unfair quota in our education system, a question was raised now and then in meetings of teachers in our school: "If a Tutsi child is allowed to study medicine, will Hutus believe that he gives lower-quality care because he is considered to be a lower-quality person? Or whatever other course of studies he takes, will he do sub-standard work after receiving his diploma?" Painful thoughts that clearly reflected how most of the population regarded Tutsis.

Talented Tutsi youths did not have the chance to continue their studies and had to earn their livings another way, for example as chauffeurs. For them, it was one more reason to leave the country and try their luck elsewhere. In Uganda they often joined the RPF. We never saw them again. My husband's youngest brother sought his fortune in another neighbouring country, Burundi, and finished his studies there.

A positive side of the Habyarimana government was that a time of relative peace began, a time when people had the chance, within the given circumstances, to develop themselves according to their own capacities. Everyone had the freedom to more or less live his own life, to practice his professions or find his own way to make an income. Some went into stockbreeding or agriculture; others found their happiness in neighbouring countries. It was possible to earn an honest living.

In spite of the period of calm that Rwanda experienced thanks to Habyarimana, the Tutsis still lived in fear of being threatened or even murdered. They were dependent on which way the political wind was blowing and what the government's mood was at any given moment. Even in 1973 there was never any fuss when a Tutsi was murdered, and the murderers were never prosecuted.

And also people began to get the idea that Tutsis were not Rwandans but strangers, foreigners, aliens from Ethiopia who had immigrated to Rwanda. That was how the government as well as many Hutus regarded the Tutsis. These new concepts were accepted as the undisputed truth and inscribed in the national history of Rwanda. It was part of what led to the ethnic quota. So it was no wonder that a contemptuous and disdainful attitude towards Tutsis predominated in education.

I speak from experience about the discriminatory limit on admission to secondary education because during the twenty-four years I worked as a teacher, I had to fill out a list at the beginning of every school year. Every teacher noted down the number of Hutu, Tutsi and Twa boys and girls in his or her class. As a teacher you would go and stand in front of the class and ask each child about his or her ethnic origin, which very quickly made the children aware that there were ethnic differences among them.

The question of mixed marriages, or marriages between Hutu and Tutsi, was especially sad and painful for me. In our culture the father determines the child's lineage. Children became confused. After the list was drawn up, they left the class asking each other in surprise: "Your father and my mother are brother and sister, but you're Hutu and I'm Tutsi!"

Children grew up in an atmosphere of contradiction and not in the very important spirit of national unity. From their first day at school, they were made aware at a very young age of the differences between them, and this would create conflicts between the two groups later on. This attitude towards difference made it very easy for the government to separate people into those who must be killed and those who must do the killing. It also meant that lists with the names of Tutsis predestined for murder when the right moment came could be compiled in a legal and efficient way.

Envy also played a role in the making of these lists. Tutsis who had possessions and were well off were quickly accused of maintaining relations with their relatives in neighbouring countries; it was rumoured that family members were conspiring together to overthrow the Rwandan government.

All of those lists would make it easy to track people down during the genocide. We received advance warning of these premeditated murder plans from my sister Rosalie, because she could already name names of people on the death list.

At that time already, in the unrest of 1973, Hutus were going from house to house deliberately looking for Tutsis to plunder, destroy and kill. The genocide was planned and took partial form that year.

Even in the school where I worked, it was clear who was a Hutu teacher and who was a Tutsi teacher. Even if there were no problems among the teachers, during the riots one was in significant danger of being killed by a colleague; friendships suddenly ceased to exist during conflicts. Colleagues of mine joined Hutu groups and set about plundering and murdering. The reason for these violent outbursts was the rumour that Tutsis from surrounding countries were preparing to invade Rwanda and seize power here. In 1959 we all still believed in one future, but after the 1970s the violence was so severe and was being carried out in such a systematic, threatening way that many Tutsis left Rwanda for safety reasons.

In the most ruthless way, we learned a few years later how disastrous the implications of this politics of ethnic segregation were and where they would ultimately lead us.

THE BIRTH OF MY CHILDREN

Vigilance was still required in the years following 1973, although daily life had a certain peace and stability to it. But we could never shake the feeling of fear and mistrust. Life went on for us, myself included.

In 1978 I got engaged to Placide Rucyahana, son of Jean Baptiste Gafaranga and Annonciata Mutumwinka. My parents graciously agreed to his request for my hand in marriage. He had built his own house in Kabagari, in the former Masango district, and our marriage was consecrated on July 5th, 1978.

After all the ceremonies and festivities were over, we went to live in Kabagari and I began to teach at the local primary school. Placide worked in education too. He was the principal at two primary schools: the one in Murama, where his office was, and the school in Kerezo. He would get on his motorbike early in the morning and ride to one or the other school.

We led a quiet and happy life in our new hometown, which quickly bore fruit with the birth of our first daughter whom we named Germaine Uwishimye and nicknamed Joyeuse Ceci as an expression of our joy and happiness.

A year later we had another daughter, Claudette Umugwaneza, whose name also conveyed our sense of wellbeing.

Then, in 1981, we moved from Kabagari to Nyanza.

Our third child was born there in 1983 and we named him Dieudonné Rucyahana: his first name stood for the goodness and mercy of God, who had now blessed us with a son.

Fourth in line came Denise Mwenedata, whose name means she came to the world amongst other children of the same parents. Mwenedata also means 'sibling tenderness and solidarity'.

The next child was another son called Germain Busoro Micomyiza, a name that refers to the love of our fellow man. We manifested this love by offering help to the sick and poor, including by covering certain costs for children from less privileged families in our area. Busoro is also the name of Placide's grandfather.

Olivier Mugisha was our sixth child. His name meant 'hope'. Born peacefully, with a slightly different complexion than his siblings, and dark like his aunt Placidie.

Then another boy followed, John Rutayisire Bébé, 'hero, in God's service'. He laughed a lot.

Our last child was a son named Lambert Nkurunziza, or 'good news', he was born in 1993.

We were an affluent family of distinction. We had four houses surrounded by farmland where, amongst other things, tapioca, beans and other greens grew. We grew bananas and kept a large number of cows, which produced good milk. But for rice, we could meet all of our basic needs.

As for those cows, I still remember a group of Germans who had initiated an agricultural project in our region. Because of them, we were adequately trained in the modernization and innovation of livestock farming. Our livestock produce supplemented both of our salaries, thus enabling us to raise our children without any financial issues.

I still worked at the primary school near our house so I was able to have lunch with my children at home. I had help with all of the housework: one girl helped take care of the children, another girl helped prepare meals and clean, and a boy helped look after the cattle and the chickens. So after school I had time for my children too, to help them with their homework or to teach them other practical things.

But in Rwanda in those days, you never knew what the next day would bring.

In 1990, the RPF asked president Habyarimana to allow all Tutsis who were still in Uganda to return to Rwanda in peace. However, the president refused, and so...!

On October 2nd, 1990 the mood changed. The Inkotanyi (the RPF Tutsi liberation army) launched an attack on our country from Uganda. That morning the neighbours treated us totally differently. They no longer replied to our usual daily greetings, because... we were Tutsi!

Rumors were circulating: "The Tutsis are coming back to Rwanda to claim their rights!" Spirits plummeted to a low point, shifting to intolerance and discord. People were apprehended for being 'ibyitso' (traitors) - and put in prison.

We heard on the radio that we were no longer allowed to congregate. Tutsis with family abroad were taken into custody. Two of my uncles, Rubuguza and Kanyemera, lived in Uganda and one of Placide's uncles had moved to Tanzania a long time ago, which meant that we ended up on a blacklist.

People on the notorious lists that circulated amongst the Hutus and indicated which Tutsis had relatives living abroad, were arrested or given prison sentences. That was certainly the case for relatively well-off Tutsis. They were accused of sending money to the Inkotanyi. These were the kinds of false pretexts that were used to justify the arrest, imprisonment and even the killing of Tutsis.

A Tutsi girlfriend of ours who was married to a Hutu confirmed that my husband was on such a list. She came to secretly inform me that a list was circulating and that Placide was number three on it. She also revealed that Jean Nepomuscène Ruterana was right at the top, because his boys had fled in 1973. Theoneste Gakeri was number two because his son Rutaba had also immigrated to Uganda to join the Inkotanyi. Ruterana and Gakeri were also rich farmers who both owned quite large estates.

It became clear to us that repression was to be expected, and so we needed to stay particularly alert. This scary suspicion was confirmed a few days later when the police came and searched our houses. The agents searched for alleged weapons which we didn't have, and even though nothing suspicious was found, we remained suspects.

Some unstable years followed: sometimes it was very calm, sometimes the tension grew. Then there was a revival of violence, followed shortly thereafter by a truce. People died under mysterious circumstances but the reason for their death and the perpetrators remained suspiciously vague. Some Tutsis were imprisoned on false accusations or accused of collaborating with the RPF. Those who were arrested were treated badly in the police cell or prison, were not fed properly and were even forced to drink out of their own shoes.

Tutsis with a decent supply of possessions or a successful business were in particular danger of being accused or assaulted. Every year many Tutsis fled Rwanda, especially if they were in danger of being killed. Most of them immigrated to Uganda, where they organized themselves in a way that they hoped would enable them to return to Rwanda again peacefully some day.

We could sense that the situation was about to get out of hand. Tensions grew and we could tell that they were already looking for ways to wipe us, the Tutsis, out. Politics became even more impartial, favouring the Hutus. There was still only one party in Rwanda, the pro-Hutu MRND.

The United Nations heard that a massacre was underway and tried to turn the tide by demanding that Habyarimana rule more democratically. The government was supposed to allow for more political parties and to offer more cooperation with the Tutsis abroad as well as those in Rwanda.

These recommendations resulted in the Arusha Treaty, which was signed on August 4th, 1993. But the signatories signed with their pens and not with their hearts.

This treaty gave rise to an unprecedented, bloody genocide from which the violence that was subcutaneously brewing would barbarously burst forth, giving birth to a devastating monster.

Placide and I engage in 1978.

Placide and I marry in 1978.

Our daughter Claudette at high school.

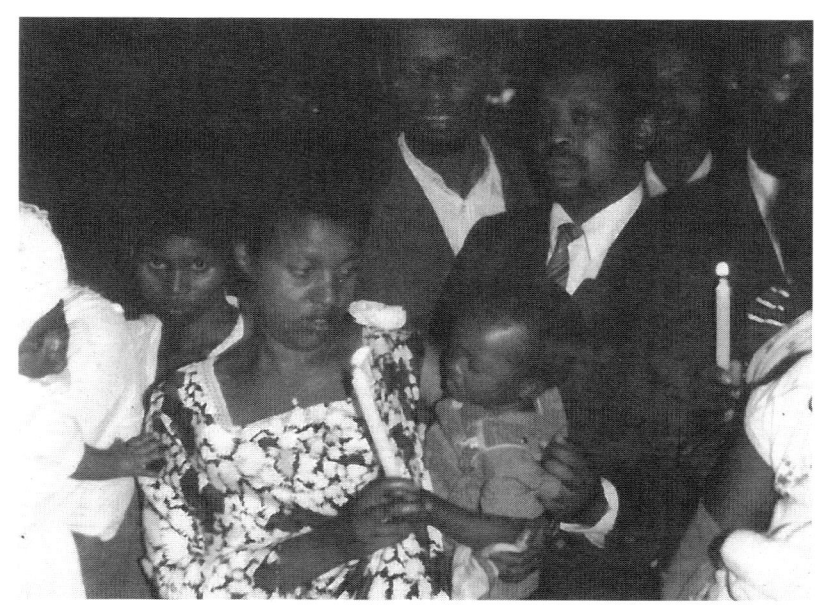

Baptism of our son Olivier.

Baptism of our son Lambert by pastor Furaha.

The last festive gathering with the whole family in 1992.

THE FIRST DAYS OF THE GENOCIDE

The seventh of April, 1994. My hands tremble as I write this. The seventh of April, a Thursday. I was at home because school was closed for Easter vacation. Thursday, the seventh of April, was the catastrophic day the dark clouds of approaching disaster gathered above us.

The mood on our hill, usually so cheerful, had changed to hostility, and you could feel the tension in the air. There was a threatening atmosphere. Normally all of our neighbours would greet us, wishing us good morning or good day. But now! I saw only grim faces that looked at me angrily, and acquaintances who turned away from me. "Good morning" I said, but some of them replied with vicious mockery: "Just wait and see if it's a good day for you!"

Surprise and fear ran through me as I wondered what in God's name could be happening. But I would learn quite soon what it was.

President Habyarimana's airplane had gone down over Kigali that night and neither he nor any of the other passengers had survived the accident. Malicious tongues spread the rumour that the plane had been shot out of the air. The radio was now spreading its poisonous hatred throughout the country in a heated, inflammatory voice, urging all Hutus to arm themselves, to set up barriers, "... to let no cockroach escape." Dangerous, life-threatening language.

Mocking songs about Tutsis echoed throughout Rwanda, followed by an urgent call for all military personnel, police and Interahame to 'go to work'. And all the aggression was turned against us, the Tutsis. The whole place buzzed with rumours: in Kigali they were murdering already, and a new president was supposed to have been appointed.

Suddenly it came home to me that my life, our lives, were at risk and that the situation was critical; death was lying very close by in wait for us.

That was proved later in the day by the panicky chaos of a turbulent crowd of displaced people, large groups of Tutsis walking slowly over the surrounding hills that Thursday, driving cows and goats before them. I learned that they were fleeing the famous Gikongoro, which was one of the twelve prefectures of Rwanda at that time.

All of these people needed help urgently and we did our best to provide food for them as they came through, and I noticed that parents thought first of their children.

A week later I saw another great mass of refugees come by, now coming from Murama and Masango, two communes belonging to the prefecture of Gitarama. Other groups of Tutsis fleeing from Musange and Bwakira joined this group.

Flare-ups of violence had driven them out of their homes. They had already survived several attacks on their flight here but others from their villages and regions had not been so lucky, falling victim to the murderous Hutu rage on the way. Many of these Tutsis were looking for a safe refuge in Burundi, and the road to that country ran through the province where we lived, Nyanza. Many of the refugees slept in the open air, such as on our hill, Mount Gacu. Others found shelter with relatives or acquaintances. Students sought out fellow students.

In the region from which these Tutsis came, the 'bourgmestres' had already acted, inciting people to kill as many Tutsis as possible. But our mayor had forbidden the residents of Nyanza to take part in the massacres. Unfortunately he later paid for that with his own life. He was bound behind a car and dragged through the streets of Nyanza as an example to others of the fate they could expect if they did not do as instructed. After that, the slaughters began in our area, although later here than elsewhere in Rwanda.

On April 18th the interim president Theodore Sindikubwabo visited the city of Butare, a town a little south of Nyanza, and addressed a gathering of the mayors of the region. I heard the speech over the radio and still remember one sentence that stood out for me: "I note that there are Hutus who feel this does not concern them very much and who do not want to take part in these actions!"

His words left us with no hope at all. After his speech, the interim president called the mayors of the prefecture Gitarama together and gave them instructions. The mayors met in turn with the town councillors to emphasize the extremely important purpose of the actions, and to mobilize them for the massacres.

At first many Hutus in the south refused to take part in the massacres, but the fierce campaigns with their inflammatory, threatening language finally convinced them to drop their objections and choose to take part in the slaughter.

Although in some regions of the country, the cold-blooded murder of Tutsis began immediately on April 7th, in our area Nyanza, the first acts of bloody violence occurred on April 21st. But even on that day, Hutus hesitated to kill their Tutsi neighbours because they felt they would be doing things that were against their conscience by taking actions they could not stand behind.

From the beginning, intellectual Hutus did their very best to encourage and incite not only well educated bystanders, but also ordinary people against Tutsis, to encourage them to murder. They told these people, who were often poor, that in this way they could compensate for their unemployment by seizing and dividing up Tutsi possessions.

In spite of all that, doubt and confusion still reigned in Nyanza over whether or not to take part. The unrest grew greater and it brought many of the people out on the streets, but the mood changed drastically when a section of the gendarmerie (military police) arrived. They were charged with initiating the hunt for Tutsis. In the center, bursts of gunfire suddenly reverberated, coming from these agents. They fired in the air and that frightening sound alarmed everyone, driving Hutus and Tutsis apart. Everyone ran in all directions, to the suburbs, to friends, to the hills around us to find refuge there, anywhere to get away from those agents that continued shooting in the air. I was at home on April 21st and since we lived a short distance from the center of Nyanza, I observed it all from close by.

One day after this incident, the councillors called on all Hutus to return quietly to their homes.

Two days later, a group of youths, including a certain Kabanda with his two brothers Paul Ukobizaba and Bwanamudogo (or Joseph Mukasa Ukobizaba), together with a former soldier and council member, Rurangwa, held a meeting. Rurangwa persuaded the youths to throw up a barrier, a roadblock, at a few little shops next to a wide sand road running outside of Nyanza. It was a strategic point where five roads and paths crossed, and from there they could block all Tutsi traffic. Every passerby had to show his identity card and have his identity checked by the Interahamwe. This card with a photograph on it, some personal information and the specification of Hutu, Tutsi or Twa (a distinction introduced in 1931 by the Belgians) made it very easy to identify and kill Tutsis. From this location, 'Centre Progrès', the genocide now spread to Remera and Mpanga and revealed its deadly character.

The placement of the barrier was a conscious choice. It was central to an area where many Tutsis lived, especially those belonging to the great Abagamba and Abanyoni clans. By blocking this high road, the genocidaires could be sure that no one could escape them. And they were almost completely successful in carrying out their plan, although a few did survive their murderous violence.

There was hustle and bustle around this slovenly roadblock of stones and branches. There was dancing, people jumped around, shrill whistles sounded. Aggressive youths, some with bare upper bodies, wearing banana leaves around their waists and red bands on their arms, chanted "Hutu power!" and "Death to all Tutsis!" They sang mean, scurrilous songs to mock Tutsis.

They were often overgrown boys, out of work, who had few chances in life and so hung around here and there. They were bored and up to all kinds of tricks. I knew them well. It was easy to get them to go along with violence. Yes, of course they participated! And how! What was holding them back? Who was in a position to put an end to the perilous threat there? Did we all have to die first?

The situation in Nyanza began to get out of hand and my family and I found ourselves in a tense, threatening atmosphere. After April 21st, it was really no longer sensible to sleep at home.

The first night we stayed with a family that was friends of Bernard Munyabitare. They belonged to the Abagamba clan. Frida, the daughter of Bernard, was a good friend of mine. That night we prayed together for a good outcome, that we would all survive the violence. The next day, we found good Hutu friends who were prepared to take in three of our children. I sheltered with Bernard's family, with the four youngest. I stayed overnight there and the next day, alone with Lambert now, I went back to our house where Placide had stayed with our son Dieudonné and three servants.

In the meantime, I learned of the devilish plans that had been laid for my husband's family. The initiators, the planners, wanted to eradicate that whole family, young and old, in order to provoke the Hutus, who were very fond of Placide, into taking part. The malicious plotters intended to discourage them so that later they could convince them - or force them - to take part in violence against Tutsis.

We had always been friendly and helpful to everyone; we shared our milk, our juice, vegetables and clothes. Sometimes, we even gave away a cow. We found people work, sometimes money. For some, we paid for their education. We even helped some of them get their driver's licenses, like Rusinga. So we helped people that way and they were very grateful. After the genocide I heard reactions to the death of their benefactor, Placide. Our neighbour Emmanuël was so angry that he grabbed a machete and shouted "Placide is dead! I'm going to smash everyone I meet!"

And so when I heard about that treacherous, devilish plan, I knew I couldn't wait any more to get my children to safety. Preferably as far as possible from home, because the leaders wanted to set an example by destroying Placide's family, to push people in the region into more mass killing.

Early in the morning, I came back to that little shopping center, 'Centre Progrès', where the infamous roadblock closed off our path. There I met Paul, whose mother Thérèse was a colleague of mine. She was a Tutsi, unlike her husband and children who were Hutus. We got along very well. Placide and I regularly went to their parties and her oldest daughter was a good friend of my daughter. I dared to speak to Paul.

"Why is this barrier here?" I asked.

This was done, he explained, to protect the people against an attack by the Inkotanyi and to hold them off here if necessary. I looked to the side and saw his brother-in-law standing there, Jean Damascene Dirimas, who visited his mother-in-law in Nyanza every now and then and whose high position commanded respect and admiration from everyone in Kigali. He had returned from the capital shortly after the genocide broke out, to stir up aggression here and to convince as many Hutus as possible to take part in eradicating Tutsis.

He stood with a thick notebook in his hands, very self-important and surrounded by six youths. I called one of them over and asked him to go with me, because I didn't trust the situation and was afraid. Potien was the boy's name. He was Placide's cousin because their mothers were sisters. Potien confided to me that at the barrier they were busy making a list of Tutsis on whom they would carry out their murderous attacks, and he could not hide from me that we were on the list and that it would be our turn soon.

I felt very anxious and asked him to let me through. That was no problem and with Potien I quickly went to a place where I thought I would meet Placide. He had gone to get his hair cut with Bernard. Upset, I told him what I had learned. Placide immediately asked Potien to run to his parents' house to get the motorcycle that he had left there. Placide knew that there were people walking around stealing the benzene from cars and motorcycles to set Tutsi houses on fire. That had been successfully tested on houses in Eurade and Nyirakarema. They poured stolen benzene on banana leaves, lit them and threw them into or onto houses.

In the meantime, I hurried home to quickly give all kinds of orders. I told those who tended the cows to milk them and give all the milk to the refugees who had sought protection with us, at least for as long as the animals had not yet been slaughtered and the refugees had not yet been murdered.

I told my mother and father-in-law, my sister-in-law and Placidie, Placide's cousin, as well as Janvier, Placidie's child, and other young people from Nyanza to find milk and food for themselves. I gave them what I could and emphasized again that now they must look out for themselves. I took money with me because I thought I might need it in my flight.

I said goodbye with pain in my heart. Leaving was hard and caused me much grief, and tears streamed over my cheeks. I advised the girl who was looking after the children to go home so that she wouldn't be killed on my account, even though she was a Hutu. She refused indignantly and swore to me that she would stay with the children, and she also wanted to take care of everyone else who was still in the house. She even offered to take Lambert, whom I was carrying on my back, and hide him with her family. This I resolutely rejected and I made it clear that I would keep my youngest child with me, wherever I was, in life but if I had no other choice, until death.

Going back in the direction of Bernard, towards the shelter where I had slept the night before, I had to go by that horrible barrier again, where hulking men had already held back a number of people and driven them together in a group. Among them was a former seminarian. This candidate for the priesthood was beaten hard with a whip after they had seen from his identity card that he was a Tutsi. He had tried to find a place to stay in the parish of Nyanza, but there were no priests left there because they had all fled to a safer place. They searched him and someone found a large envelope he was carrying. They lashed him harder and another youth struck him hard with a stick because they suspected him of carrying grenades.

A few men turned toward me with angry looks and asked where I was going. I shuddered and answered timidly that I was going back to Bernard where I had slept that night, to pick up my children that I had left there. They commanded me to walk through quickly, otherwise there was a good chance that I wouldn't come back alive.

I hurried away as fast as I could from that terrible place, because I saw that a brooding and poisonous atmosphere was already hanging over the blockade. You could see it clearly in the faces, the red eyes of the councillor Rurangwa and his friends Paul, Dirimas, Elia, Sabagirirwa and all the others. They whispered a few names among themselves and waved their machetes and spears threateningly in the air a few times.

A little farther on I came across the Hutu trader Japhet, who was on his way to a roadblock located further on, in Musoni. The local leaders of the MRND held meetings there.

Where was I going, he asked rudely, shamelessly. I reacted angrily "Where are you going?" But he warned me threateningly and in a loud voice that I would not escape my fate, no matter where I ran.

I walked quickly on and came upon a crowded street full of fleeing people: tired old men and women with children who walked in front of them, crying. Then the terrible reality sank in deeper. I felt that the end was now so near.

I walked on to a corner and came upon another roadblock that, to my great dismay, kept me away from Bernard, where I had left my children. Feeling hunted, I walked to the house of Feliciën,

Donatille's husband, a Tutsi. I was just going to tell him that I had passed the barrier of 'Centre Progrès' at the risk of my life, when a girl rushed into the courtyard in a panic. I recognized Mukamana, the daughter of Maruveri. This Maruveri, an older man, had just been shot dead by the gendarmes, who were trying to intimidate the population and were shooting everyone mercilessly and unceremoniously if they did not obey at once. Mukamana told us brokenly that at the barrier she had heard the notorious Paul tell his older brother Kabanda that they were going to kill people and burn their houses, beginning with all the intellectual men and the traders. That Paul had also emphasized that they must not forget to slaughter the cows as a reward for all their work, to regain their strength and finish what they had started in 1959.

After that macabre disclosure, Mukamana looked around desperately and then ran out again. I do not know what happened to her, but I am convinced that she lost her life. Upset, I sat halfway up the hill before Feliciën's door and did not know where to go. I realized that I could not return to Bernard because of the blockade.

Hopelessly, I peered at the roadblock and suddenly saw, ten meters farther up, my son Germain followed by two of Bernard's children, running past. They were returning from herding cows and on their way to Bernard's. Since there was a lot of killing going on at the other roadblock of 'Centre Progrès', Feliciën and I shouted that it was dangerous to pass the barricade below. The boys saw us and walked more slowly, and called to us that children could just go through. My son turned to me, put his sweater on his head, raised his arm and waved goodbye to me: "Goodbye, Mama!" I called to him with my whole soul that I would do my best to see him again that evening. Tragically, I did not see him again until his dead body was buried, after the end of the genocide. I can't let go of the image of him waving goodbye. It will never leave my heart. I will carry his last farewell with me all my life.

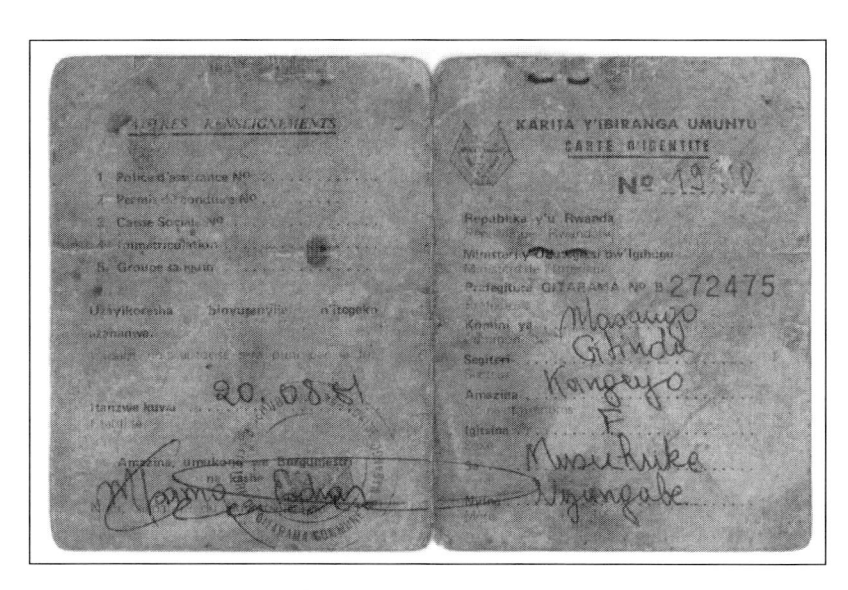

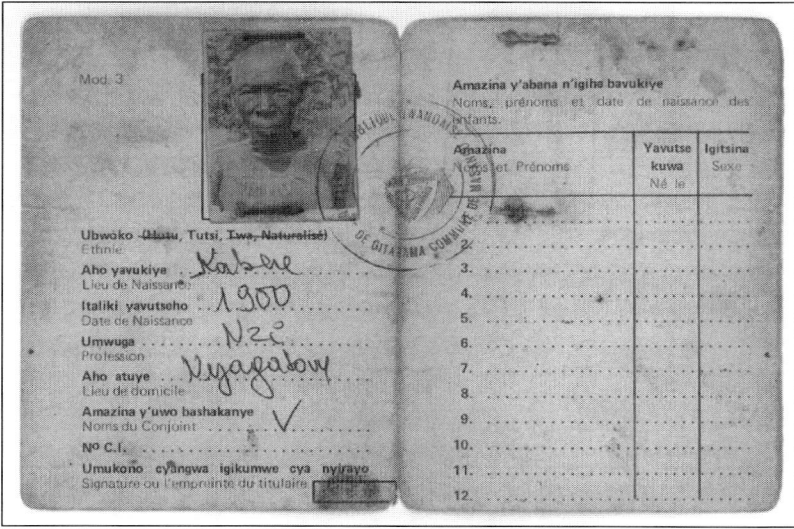

Identity card of my grandmother. The mentioning of Hutu, Tutsi and Twa in the identity cards made it easy for the murderers to identify Tutsis and to kill them.

ON THE RUN

Shortly after Germain disappeared out of sight, the terrible sound of shrill and urgent whistles sent me fleeing in panic. As I fled with Lambert still on my back, I ran into my nieces, Alexia and Gloriose, who lived with me. Terrified, we deliberated for a moment and then I ran with them to the other side of the hill where Evariste, a young man who traded in Nyanza, lived. Lambert and I and my nieces were warmly welcomed. I am still so grateful to Evariste's sister for staying with the girls and I all night long and suggesting, or rather urging us to pray together, in the hope that, should we die, we would all go to heaven.

Thoroughly upset, she told me about the Hutus' terrible plans; they had sworn that no Tutsi would be spared. She wasn't in a good position either, since she was a Hutu woman married to a Tutsi man. According to the law, her children were Tutsi, so she had had the foresight to send them to live with her father. He served as a prominent soldier in the government army. Her other brothers were prominent members of the Interahamwe; terribly brutal men who had already killed many Tutsis and who showed no mercy. I can't understand how such an enormously kind woman could have such brutal men as brothers. Evariste's sister later literally fell ill from all the misery around her and died merely from having witnessed such horrific violence.

One of her brothers came to visit and started to list the names of Tutsis who were suspected of having weapons in their homes. Among them he named Gahamanya, Gloriose and Alexia's father, my husband Placide, as well as Bernard who had sheltered me on my last night with my children. These would be the first families to be captured and murdered. Also listed were Mugabowishema, Rusanganwa the trader, and the vetenarians Panda and Nyerere. The next morning the young man Evariste urged me to find refuge somewhere else because his brothers had discovered the hiding place in his house. But his sister begged him to let me stay there. She tried to persuade Evariste not to send me away by arguing that the baby was an extra handicap for me. She said that the small child would make it so much harder for me to hide safely. But there was no doubt in Evariste's mind. He was convinced that we would all be killed indiscriminately.

Suddenly, Catherine, my neighbour Rwatamanywa's daughter, ran screaming into the yard, totally beside herself, quickly followed by Pauline, Gafiligi's daughter. Crying, she screamed desperately: "Help! Help me! They've set everything on fire, they're killing everyone! We're going to die too!!" Evariste was so scared now that he forced the girls and us to leave the house immediately.

Pauline and Catherine left the house utterly distressed. After the genocide I saw Pauline again and she told me that Catherine and her family had been massacred. She was also the one who later told me that my husband Placide was dead. Gafiligi and her brother had not escaped their fate of death either.

But Evariste had sent Lambert and me away too. Where were we supposed to go? I had no idea. At first I just started wandering aimlessly with Alexia and Gloriose. Finally, I chose the path up the hill to Mpanga, a forest of pine trees. The girls thought a path down along a pea field would be better. With tears in my eyes, I said goodbye to Alexia and Gloriose: "We will see each other again in heaven."

I wasn't the only one hoping to find a safe dwelling in the thick Mpanga forest; lots of other Tutsis had gathered there too, seeking refuge from near and far.

I needed to sleep. The fatigue was dragging me down. I kept asking myself: when will it be my turn, when will they catch us? Or will this terrible misery at long last end? Poor Lambert. Maybe I'd have some time to take care of him and be able to give him some attention now. My thoughts turned to my children and to Placide. Not knowing their fate stirred up the turmoil inside me.

It stayed quiet that week in any event, and we didn't have to suffer from the cold or go hungry.

But soon thereafter, I think it was the 2nd of May, I experienced one of the first dark days of my life. Once again, the sharp and frightful whistles sounded all around. Terrifying shrieks and rhythmic chants filled the air. "We're going to kill you! We're going to kill you! We're going to wipe you out!"

From behind the trees I saw a wild mob of leaping and howling men, as they surged down from Rushoka hill near Musoni's barrier, like a gang unleashed. A mix of coloured shirts and t-shirts quickly spread all over the hillside, contrasting unnaturally with the peaceful green scenery.

They swayed like madmen with their shiny new machetes shimmering and flashing frightfully in the sunlight. They all moved our way, on the hunt for Tutsis hiding in the trees and bushes.

I knew from spending that week with my peers in the forest that Muslims in nearby Mugandamure had been hiding fellow Muslims in their mosque. When they saw the advancing gang, the Muslims amongst us tried to leave the forest as quickly as possible to flee towards Mugandamure.

Other Tutsis dove right and left into bushes or ran away as fast as they could, hoping they could escape death. I could hear relentless, desperate screaming, Tutsis weeping in terror, hunted down or discovered. They were slaughtered one by one. The younger amongst us broke into a run. I ran with them, but it's not easy running with a child on your back, so I had to drop back. An old Hutu man standing in the path further up made me stop. I begged him to let me by, but he stood his ground. What gave him the right to stop me? The thought triggered anger, which rose up inside me. I stated my defence, declaring that God would punish him if he stopped me. He let me pass with visible reluctance, snapping viciously that others would manage to find me. I ran quickly past, escaping my persecutors.

ISAAC AND HIS PREDICTION

A little further along, panting, I slipped into the courtyard of an old Hutu man. I saw him as he was putting his shoes on. He was grumbling out loud to someone I couldn't see that he was often disturbed by noise right when he wanted to pray. Also, from his mumbled words I was able to make out that he had vowed never to kill anyone. It later turned out that he was an Adventist.

Encouraged by his words, I stepped into his house and asked him expectantly if I could hide out there. "They're looking for me and my child. They're going to kill us. I've been on the run for days." And, as if to prove it to him, I told him the whole story of my flight. I noted a trace of doubt in his eyes. He scrutinised me, but my miserable experiences made such an impression on him that I eventually persuaded him to allow me to use his home as a hiding place, but on condition that if I was discovered, I would not let on that he had given his permission.

The man introduced himself as Isaac and he lived in the house with his daughter. He behaved like a true Christian because he began to pray not only for me, but also for the murderers, that they might come to repent. After his prayer he stepped into the courtyard where he ran into a group of belligerent men. They wanted to know if he was hiding Tutsis in his house, but the old man made out that he didn't understand why they were asking him that. Tutsis? No, he wouldn't even allow them into his home, let alone offer them shelter. No, they wouldn't find any Tutsis under his roof. He was angry and to his words he added a wise proverb: "You shall reap what you sow!"

That didn't go down well and the men began insulting him in all ways imaginable. They cursed him, swore at him but they didn't force their way into his house.

When they had gone, he showed me to the banana plantation and advised me to hide out there, because he had a sneaking suspicion that they were going to come back to murder me and my child after all.

At nightfall I quietly crept to the plantation. In the middle there were taro plants growing. Little Lambert and I were able to hide under their big leaves. We slept there undisturbed for almost four hours before we were startled awake by shouting men with bloodthirsty screams who were chasing a cow that had escaped from the slaughterhouse.

The cow and its pursuers all ran straight through the plantation. They passed so close by us. In fact, they almost fell over us but they didn't notice us. And the cow? It escaped.

That we were not discovered, I still don't understand. I can only explain it as a miracle from the Almighty.

As soon as the men had disappeared from sight, I ran quickly into Isaac's house. He was irritated and asked me why I had come back. "Stay in the banana plantation!" Nevertheless, he first sent his daughter to get milk and then told her to walk back with us to the banana plantation where she was to cover us with leaves. Shortly afterwards one of the members of the mob came back and started searching among the leaves, hacking with his machete. Slowly, closer and closer, looking around carefully and with swiping motions, he approached our hiding place. I held my breath and hoped to God that Lambert would keep quiet. The man stood still and was now standing so close that I could hear his mumbling and even his breathing, but luckily he shuffled slowly away in the direction of the courtyard where he found some ripe passion fruit. After a few minutes he ran away, thank God. We were saved! We'd survived again.

The blasted man had barely left when a young man - I reckoned him to be about 17 years old - approached me cautiously and asked if I was also a Tutsi since I was hiding. He had fled from Kibuye, only dared to travel by night and kept himself out of sight during the day. The poor boy felt so tired, was so totally exhausted, that he had given up all hope of ever reaching Burundi. He had seen the most terrible things in Kibuye.

"Maman, they killed the children, they raped women and girls, they even murdered the old people." He fell silent for a moment and then began again: "They killed my mother. Our youngest, a one-month-old baby, was beaten to death on the ground." He looked at me, full of fear: "Maman, they killed priests, you know, they killed the pastor." He was silent again but, overcome by such strong emotion, he felt compelled to share his terrible story with me. Still in shock, he stammered as he spoke about how he had escaped the massacre of the group of Tutsis that he'd been on the run with. All around him many of his people had been killed, literally hacked into pieces. Blood, blood and more blood, flowing over the roads. He had also taken a beating, but wasn't wounded. He had stumbled and had lain on the ground while one mutilated body after another had fallen on top of him. For two days he'd kept still under those dead bodies and had then seen a chance to wriggle his way out and escape. Time and again he had seen the blood flowing. Even in his sleep he was still tormented by the sight of all that blood. He crept further into the banana plantation to find a safe place.

Early in the morning a group of killers, who had already wreaked havoc on the hill, came closer by. They yelled out: "We've searched every house in Mpanga and we heard that there are still people hiding out here that we haven't found yet.

We know you're here! Come out! Come here!"

With shrill whistles and loud shouting they now began to search.

Those deceitful words again: "Yes, come on! We have seen you! Come here! Come on, you'd better come out now or you're just going to make it worse for yourselves!" The boy whose story I have just told was so convinced they had discovered him that he emerged from his hiding place.

"Are there more cockroaches there?" He shook his head. "No." They grabbed hold of him. I can still see him before me, such a young lad. I can't forget him. He didn't give me away, in spite of his fear. That must have taken such a lot of courage.

I pressed myself hard against the ground. I heard the boy desperately begging the killers to spare him, because his family had already been completely wiped out and with all the misery he'd been through he would soon die from the sorrow anyway. But they took no notice of his words and they started to beat him and hack at him with their machetes. Those that had stones threw stones at him and those with spears used their spears. The boy was slaughtered by every last one of that frenzied mob. With a last cry he called out in his agony that he was innocent and was being killed only because of his ethnicity. But he was going to denounce them to the Almighty. His voice broke then and it went quiet. Only the triumphant chanting of "Hutu power! Hutu power!" resounded across the plantation. I heard one of the Hutus proudly declare that the boy was the one hundredth Tutsi that he had killed. This was rewarded with cheers. "Hutu power! Hutu power!"

Then they left, the barbaric devils, having finished their work: the slaughter of a young man.

Having witnessed this dehumanising crime from my hiding place, I felt my body stiffen. My body became ice cold and an incredible nauseous feeling came over me. I was devastated. My heart skipped and it rose up through my body as if it wanted to leave through my mouth. I trembled and choked. Tears flowed over my cheeks. Then I felt Lambert's nails dig firmly into my back as if to say: "Come on, we have to get out of here!"

When I stood up and tried to walk to Isaac's house, my strength gave out and I fell to the ground. After they'd gone, Isaac's daughter came outside to see if I'd been killed. The young woman was extremely surprised to see me alive and considered it a miracle that I had not been killed. She helped me to my feet and took us with her into the house and showed us to a place where we could hide. Before we slept, she prayed with her father to thank God for sparing our lives.

Early the next morning we heard the killers in the distance shouting fiercely as they returned. Isaac urgently advised me to leave the hill. But where was I to go? I wanted to stay with the family and preferred to die there with them and to be buried by them. Isaac eventually managed to convince me that it was better to leave, but wanted to say a prayer before I left.

Praying out loud, he lay his hands on my head and on Lambert's little head and he told me to arm myself with the Bible which he then handed to me. "But I already have a rosary!" I refused it but he insisted I use the book as a shield against death, as protection for me and for my child. I asked him to continue to pray for us, that we would survive and that we Tutsis would not be wiped from the face of the earth.

"You shall not die; your child shall not die. I shall not die and my daughter shall not die either. My family shall not die, but the murderers shall be held to account for their deeds. We shall see each other again in this life when the killing has ended."

His words have remained with me and I remember this scene as if it was yesterday.

As I was leaving, the daughter suggested I leave my son with them so that they could look after him and take care of him. I refused and told them: "If I survive, I survive with my child. If I die, I die with my child."

Isaac and his daughter accompanied me to the road and wished me peace. Isaac pushed the small Bible into my hands, but I refused, was insulted even. Indignantly and angrily, I asserted that the Bible was not a grenade I could throw at my pursuers, nor was it a machete I could swing about me should my enemy come too close. If I could provoke the anger of the killers with my resistance, then they would just have to kill me quickly. With a hint of sarcasm, I observed: "And if books can protect me and are so important, then I wouldn't have had any problems at all the last few weeks. Then I would have lugged all the books from home along with me."

I reminded Isaac once again that I'd come here looking for a hiding place and didn't want to be fobbed off with his wisdom that a book, that a Bible, is the answer. And certainly not when I hadn't even been able to immerse myself in that book, the Bible. But Isaac did not accept my response and slipped the book into the shawl that I'd used to strap Lambert to my back.

Not only did he give me the Bible, but also an emphatic prediction: "You shall see that the Bible carries within it a strength that will strengthen you. We shall see each other again after these dark days."

WILL IT NEVER STOP!

Lambert and I left Isaac's house feeling depressed. I hobbled along with difficulty. My feet were very stiff as I'd hardly walked for days. Less than fifty metres from the house, I met a man who looked at me and sneered. He started sniggering and said: "Hey, I've been looking for an inyenzi. And now look!"
I immediately heard Isaac's voice behind me. He angrily forbade the shedding of any blood and told the man to let me pass freely. The man in question turned out to be Isaac's son.
So where to? I just headed off in any direction. I plodded across coffee fields and straight through banana plantations. I experienced moments when I became so dizzy that I fell to the ground or rolled down an embankment. Then when I got up again, I heard Lambert's gentle whining, his sighing. A weak little voice. He dug his sharp little nails into my body, as if to say: "What on earth are you doing?"
As I descended the hillside into the valley, my ears picked up shouting from the next hill and I noticed a team of killers, chasing after a man who had fled into a sorghum field. The frightened fugitive came in my direction and crossed my path. To avoid having the murderous mob chase after me, I jumped inside a house that was still under construction and without a door, and sought out the remotest corner. Pff…, I breathed a sigh of relief as I heard the group rush past.
Not two minutes later Lambert was digging his nails into my back and when I looked round, I discovered a load of black ants crawling all over our bodies. Oh, as if I didn't have enough to

worry about already! I used my hands to try and clear away as many of the ants as possible. I was so tired and so tense, my body felt so numb, that I just didn't feel the ants biting at my fingers.

Not so far from the house the group of hunters suddenly turned back. What now? I quickly looked outside and saw a house nearby that was slightly lower. I headed in that direction. I clambered over a sort of wood shed that served as a fence and found myself in the courtyard. I pushed the door of the house open. It was clearly the house of poor people. A woman stood by a fire, a pan with meat above it. I noticed that the entire house was full of meat and a variety of vegetables, all undoubtedly stolen from Tutsis.

At that moment a man suddenly came in, dressed in rags, with two children. He saw me. "Well, aren't I the lucky one!" he sneered, "because I'm the one that gets to finish you off." Angrily and in no uncertain terms, I stated that he was the one that should be finished off, he who had robbed everything from others. He had stolen so much, much more than he'd ever owned in his whole life. The man stood there aghast but then, in anger, he grabbed hold of my arm tightly. Yet I was so angry myself that I threw him against the ground. He called out to his children to fetch his machete.

I ran outside and down to the Busogwe river, which had flooded due to the heavy rainfall that season. I was forced to search for a way up and came across several women who told me with fear in their eyes that Japhet, the notorious trafficker, who I had already run into a few days before, was back in Nyanza looking for reinforcements for the Interahamwe. We'd not finished speaking when we again heard the whistles and the shouting. I quickly climbed over the fence of a courtyard and stumbled into the house of someone I didn't know. A woman came over to see what was going on and noticed my child, who was sighing and whining on my back. Fortunately, she was not hostile to us. She advised me to take Lambert off my back so that he could eat. But Lambert refused and didn't want to be removed from my back. Behind me I heard a noise and when I turned around a large man, who was covered from head to toe in blood, came in. I screamed in fear and yelled that he must have killed people.

"What did you say?" he shouted in a gruff voice.

"No, no! That's not what I meant! I beg your pardon! I didn't say anything," I answered, shaken.

The fanatical hothead began telling his wife in coldblooded detail what he'd done to a number of Tutsis and from his story I understood that he had been tasked firstly with killing the men and the boys.

"And then afterwards we can have a bit of fun with the women and girls. Ha, ha, but first I'm going to have a wash!" His eyes blazed maliciously when he fixed his gaze on me, but luckily he then left the room to go and clean himself up.

His wife used this as an opportunity to get me out of the house through the dense bushes that served as a gate, leading out to the road. I crept through the bushes to the sorghum fields which stretched along the waters of the Busogwe.

I hid out there for five days. I fed myself with the green sorghum grain. My throat wasn't used to much more than that. Eating solids was almost impossible. Swallowing was difficult and painful because my throat was too dry. That's why I chewed it up very finely and I was then able to swallow the moisture that dripped out. To feed Lambert I let the moisture from the sorghum trickle from my mouth to his. As soon as it rained, I used my pinafore to collect the water that fell so that we had enough to drink. We were able to enjoy a few relatively calm days and I really hoped that those men wouldn't be bothering us anymore.

Unfortunately, on the fifth day we were rudely awoken by the familiar noise of the murderers, screaming at the top of their voices: "Finish the job, wipe out the cockroaches, down to the very last one!" At that moment I felt little Lambert's nails digging into my skin again and I thought of him as an angel warning me that if we didn't get out of there, it could well be our undoing. The enemy was approaching! Any moment now the pursuers would be in close proximity and I immediately breastfed Lambert to prevent him from crying.

With diabolical fanaticism the killers searched the bushes and sorghum fields with their sharp iron sticks. And they used that special tactic of theirs again, sowing confusion by calling out: "Hey, look, there is an inyenzi!" in the hope that a hiding Tutsi would give himself away and come out of hiding. I crept further away and tried to make myself as small as possible. My heart was racing. I took Isaac's Bible, because I had a thought: "if Isaac is so very convinced that the Bible serves as a shield and protection, how in heaven's name can God live up to that?" At the moment that this thought shot through my mind, one of the killers jumped over me and shouted: "Yes, there! An inyenzi!" One of his mates came over now as well and shouted: "Yes, there he is!" Huddled up with my eyes shut tight, I waited, full of fear and tension, to see what was going to happen. Should I make a run for it? Minutes crept by. My ears pricked up and picked up every sound. I didn't dare to believe it: were the voices moving further away? Did they sound further and further away from me or did it just seem so? Cautiously I opened my eyes. Should I dare take a look yet? I dared to lift myself slowly up to see if the danger had passed. Thank God! I couldn't see them anymore! They were gone!

I struggled to my feet and I noticed then that there was blood on my left hand. During the search one of the men had stabbed me with the sharp point of his stick and I had been left with a nasty injury. That I'd not felt any pain at the moment I was stabbed was most likely due to the fear that had held me tightly in its grip.

To this very day, I am grateful to God that he blinded the killers' eyes to me and my hiding place. When I look at my hand, the deep scar still reminds me of that terrible incident. But I am aware that I had a lucky escape, because that day the killers murdered a lot of people and did not flinch from cutting the throats of many of them. "Brilliant! That's one less snake! Great, this cockroach is dead too!" The cheering, but also the screaming and shouting, the unforgettable desperate wailing of the victims condemned to death, still regularly plague my subconscious.

The brutal hunt had moved on, but the fear had robbed me of my breath. I cried for my fellow humans who had had their lives ended in such a ruthless and horrific way. I had the awful suspicion that one of my children, who had possibly also been hiding here in the bushes, was among the victims.

The slaughter went on until at a certain moment I heard a very loud voice yell: "Stop! Stop now! We've killed enough of them for today. There are certainly still people hiding around here, but we'll come back tomorrow!" He gave a blast on his whistle which meant that it was time for the murder club to reward themselves for work well done with cows and beer.

After their departure I crawled with difficulty to the riverbank, severely weakened and in pain.

I intended to cross the water, thereby preventing my pursuers from finding me and killing me the following day. The water level had risen so high, however, that I wondered how I was supposed to get across the river without incident. Crawling, I slipped down along the riverbank, trying to grasp hold of the grass. But that grass, 'urukembagafu', was so sharp that it cut my hands. Still I continued and I stepped into the rough, raging water. The water was so wild, the current so strong, that I was thrown around in all directions. With the utmost effort, as much strength as I was capable of, I swam across to the other side and was thrown down upon the other bank. As I lay there, I suddenly thought of Lambert. He was sure to have swallowed some water. In a panic I grabbed him from my back. He didn't respond. I laid him on the ground and began to press my hands on his stomach. Water came trickling out of his mouth, but a little later he was conscious again. I also quickly wrung out our clothes before we moved on so as not to lose any time. The crossing had brought us to another sector and from there we headed on our way again. Shortly afterwards I made my way through a dense undergrowth of grass, grass intended for Gatagara village's livestock to graze on. In any case, it seemed to me a very appropriate place to hide out.

We'd just sat down when I felt Lambert's nails sticking into my back. I looked around and was surprised to see that there were many caterpillars, 'ibimata', filthy and packed in clusters, squirming and crawling all over Lambert and me. These yellow-green creatures produce a sticky substance and stick to your body, while their sting causes irritation. The little creatures covered us from head to toe and gave us an uncomfortable feeling. Still I consoled myself with the thought that I'd rather be killed by these caterpillars than by the Interahamwe, because animals kill without feelings of revenge or evil intent.

I got to my feet and tried to remove the caterpillars with my hands, but that was not easy. Rain, or rather a huge downpour, eventually got rid of the creatures. I took our clothes off and I beat them dry, and I removed all the remaining caterpillars, but also took the opportunity to have a good wash and dry the clothes. I was relieved to find that my money was still there.

Lambert looked at me with his big eyes to let me know he was happy that we were free from those filthy creatures. I raised my arms to the sky and I begged God to stand by us because I sensed that my strength was at an end.

Every time I think back on those moments, the river, the caterpillars, the rain, I dare to say that God, the Great and Almighty, protected us from influenza, malaria, pneumonia and other fatal diseases that we could have acquired so much more easily in such unhealthy living conditions. Yes, I can say with certainty that I have Him to thank. That Lambert and I came out of this alive together, I consider a miracle. I have no other way to describe it.

We didn't hang around there for long and, without knowing where, we headed further up the hill. The sudden sound of yelling and shouting on the other side alerted me to the fact that our pursuers had seen us. They ran down like crazy, dove into the river and came in our direction. With my child on my back, I ran as fast as I could with the whole gang chasing after me. When I reached the other side of the hill, I saw them appear on the top of the ridge. In my hasty flight I stopped by an old man who was grazing his cows. "Lie down on the ground and I will cover you with banana leaves. With a child on your back you won't get far. They'll catch up with you in no time." But because I didn't trust him - the man could easily have been a Hutu, because how was it possible for a Tutsi to be calmly grazing his cows? - I carried on running.

The killers came running from all directions. They shouted to each other: "Get that woman with the child on her back! Stop her! And get that man with the red pants as well!" So now they were also chasing after someone else, a man with red pants. It turned out to be Grégoir, one of my neighbours. It really seemed like a hunt now, a hunt where the game is chased from one side to the other. When Grégoir heard that he'd been discovered, he immediately took off his red pants (he was wearing another underneath) and threw them away. I couldn't change my clothes because of the child I was carrying on my back. But I saw a hut where a woman was standing by the door. The woman, from a Twa pygmy family, beckoned me inside and gave me the chance to hide. She pointed me in the direction of a small hut where she kept the urns that she made by hand. I went quickly into the hut, sat behind the urns and she covered me with a wicker mat that wasn't yet finished.

I'd only just sat down when I heard shouting: "Where is that woman we saw?" The Twa woman who had let me inside, played dumb and said that she hadn't seen anyone and that that woman must have headed off towards Kiruli, a place where many Tutsis had sought refuge. In an attempt to throw the men yet further off my scent, she added insolently: "When you've found her, bring me her clothes, because I really have nothing to wear."

The intruders pushed her roughly out of the way, forced their way into her home and began turning the place upside down to find me. I heard them. "Now I've really had it!" I thought. I was distraught and crawled further away in fear of my life.

The woman couldn't suppress the jeering tone in her voice when she said: "You're giving her more time to escape now!" The savages wanted to enter the hut where I was hiding but the woman screamed: "Do not go inside that hut, because there are urns in there that I haven't finished yet. You are wasting your time and you're letting her get a head start on you!"

Coarse and clumsy guys they were and completely out of control. They ransacked the house and smashed up a lot of things in the process. Eventually they left. They hadn't entered the hut and, in my sheltered corner, I was scared to death and so upset that I wondered if I was still alive. I even had to feel on my back to see if my child was still there. I was so completely distraught that it didn't occur to me to thank the good Lord for saving me.

A little later the Twa woman came in with two bowls of thick sorghum porridge and she hoped that we would soon be warmer because we had been soaking wet from the rain and dew when we had come crashing into her home. The porridge was nice and warm, but it was difficult for me to swallow. My throat was very dry because the only thing we'd been able to drink up until now was rainwater. When Lambert had finished his bowl of porridge, I gave him mine so that he could regain his strength.

Suddenly from outside I heard a voice calling to the Twa woman that all Tutsis had been slain in a particularly thorough way. And then a young man with bloodshot eyes came inside holding a razor-sharp spear. He saw me, was taken aback for a moment, although just for a moment, because he then immediately forced me outside. I asked him to give me some time to strap my child to my back. I wanted to hide the gender of my child because Hutus slaughtered the men and the boys first.

I was no sooner standing outside when the young man pressed his spear against my neck and was about to kill me, but the Twa woman took his hand and stopped him. "Don't kill her! She will die in some other place! Do not spill human blood in my house!" I fled. I just completely lost it, I was devastated. I didn't have a clue anymore. Where was I supposed to seek refuge now this time? Dazed, I walked around and I finally ran to the bushes nearby. Looking back I saw that the man with the spear was not coming after me, but now ahead of me I saw a man coming towards me with a machete in his hand.

Not to kill me, I realised, because he didn't even ask me if I was a Tutsi. Driven by greed, he begged: "Please! Come and stand in for me at the checkpoint! They are looting Gatagara. I am afraid that the others will have taken everything by the time I get there. I will bring you back something when I return," he promised. Relieved, I answered him: "I am actually on the way to the clinic, but if you hurry I will wait here."

The checkpoint was about five hundred metres from the Twa woman's house. The man threw his machete on the ground and went to the Frippon centre for the handicapped in Gatagara. There was plenty to loot there. The area around the checkpoint looked like a battlefield. Nine bodies lay on the ground, covered in blood, naked. Their clothes had been taken from them.

I told myself to get away from there as quickly as possible. I ran into the middle of the dense forest and lay down on the ground to rest. After a while I was able to get my breath back and the tension subsided slightly. With branches and leaves, I made a bed that we could lie down on and I laid Isaac's Bible under my head.

When Lambert was lying on the bed, we looked deep into each other's eyes. Tears welled up and yet I felt reasonably calm. Nervousness, tension, exhaustion had attacked my nerves and, thanks to the stress, I couldn't form a clear image of my current situation or the dangers that threatened me. A small ray of light that kept my hope alive was pious Isaac, the old man who had predicted that we would survive. Lambert and I spent two whole days sleeping in that forest, without waking up even once. I awoke when I felt Lambert's nails in my back, for which there was always a good reason.

I lifted myself slightly and heard shots. Several rounds were fired, one after another. "This is a different sound" I whispered anxiously to myself. "Will it never stop? Are we never to get any peace? Seriously?" For a split second I entertained the thought of surrendering and letting them shoot me dead. That would be a less painful death than being killed with a machete.

People passed close by our hiding place and I heard voices telling each other that Kagwa's gun drives a lot of fugitives from their hiding places so that others can decapitate them with their machetes.

I lay down again. Saved for the time being, although it had been close. But we were still alive and we would do our best to survive on what the forest had to offer.

The calm carried my thoughts back home, to the children, to Placide, to my family. Uncertainty about what had happened to them made me afraid. "God, stand by us! Spare us from death! Allow me to see everyone alive again!"

What a desperate situation we had found ourselves in? A few weeks ago I'd still been teaching, doing sums with the children, writing exercises up on the board. And now? I've seen terrible things. This has to end at some point, doesn't it? Are we ever going to be able to live together in peace again? Is life ever going to get back to normal? Am I ever going to be in a fit state to resume my work?

I thought about Placide. He had never liked the political meetings in our commune, for example. He was very skeptical, had a bad feeling about them and therefore refused to attend them. He didn't want us to go to them either. I resented him a little for that, but perhaps he was right. They had only ever brought us this misery.

I still remember the meeting that I attended with Claudette and Joyeuse. Madame Agathe, then the minister for education, had come to address the meeting. She had called for unity without ethnic discrimination. She was a champion of good education for women and girls. Yes, that was an informative evening for us, but when I came home, Placide was livid. He was in particular angry that I'd taken the two girls with me without consulting him. We argued. I protested and explained to him that Madame Agathe's words had been an inspiration to us.

Oh, what were we getting so upset about? What is important now? Saving our sorry lives in the midst of this deadly violence, that is our primary objective. "It's getting dark now, Lambert. Let's try to sleep."

And so each day passed and the following day came, but I never knew what was just around the corner.

During the night it was my habit to go and pick little fruits ('umusagara') in the pitch black darkness and to chew them up finely to feed to Lambert. In this way at least we were able to eat something. But to my horror, in the morning light I noticed little wounds on Lambert's mouth. In the dark, I had accidentally picked the wrong fruits. I had picked the poisonous 'umumenamabuye' instead of the innocent 'umusagara.' Fortunately, it rained pretty heavily that day and that ensured there was enough water to clean the wounds. Within five days they had healed.

We stayed out there for about three weeks, in spite of the biting mosquitos and their irritating buzzing. Nevertheless, I preferred that buzzing to the dirty songs of the Interahamwe who sang: "Hutu power! Hutu power! Kill these snakes!"

THE BLACKEST DAY

Day broke, a day so terrible that I will never be able to forget it for the rest of my life.

Early in the morning I was awoken by a commotion in the distance. Shocked awake, my heart started racing. I hastily strapped Lambert to my back. His little nails clawed frantically through my clothing into the skin of my back. There was a sense of menace in the air.

There was an unholy row, as if all hell had broken loose. The killers called to each other with their loud rough voices and the shrill sound of whistles went straight through me. Criss-crossing quickly, they were getting closer and closer, shouting their inflammatory words. They raged, swore and sometimes sang. Noisily, they searched every shrub, every bush, the whole forest, thoroughly.

What could I do? I carefully lifted my head to have a look and tried to think of some way of saving us. Up until now I had always managed to escape the pursuers, sometimes as if by miracle. The shouting now came so much closer that I was able to make out fragments of words, of slogans. Familiar, hateful text. I knew them well! And then there was the high shrill sound of whistles from above. Oh, they were so many. My eyes scoured all directions to see where the threat could be coming from. In the shadow of the forest, half covered by the leaves, hidden behind branches, I tried to get a look at my pursuers. Leaves obscured my view so I pushed them aside. Careful!

God help me! Let them pass by without finding us!

They were going at it as if possessed. The calling and shouting were coming in my direction now. I listened in the direction of the invisible distance.

"Lambert, please don't make a sound! Even the slightest noise could give us away now!" But during the previous few weeks my youngest had learned only too well that making noise could bring us danger.

Up until then my strong survival instinct had helped me to keep us one step ahead of the murderers. But I could feel such fear and panic rising inside me now, feelings which paralysed me to such a degree that I doubted I could summon up the strength to keep running.

I have to be brave. I have to get us out of this. No, I will not give up!

But if they found us, I knew that we wouldn't stand a chance against this pack of wild, savage animals, prepared to horrifically slay anyone without pity in their triumphant frenzy. The most humane way to die was by the bullet. Better than having your limbs hacked off and being left to die in unbearable pain.

From all sides I heard authoritative voices and the thrashing of machetes hacking a path through the forest. Branches creaked and broke; leaves sent flying into the air rustled loudly. They were dangerously close now, ahead of me, even somewhere behind me; wildly fanatical behind their wildly fanatical machetes. They talked, laughed and breathed excitedly.

The blood rushed through my body, my thoughts were racing. I pressed myself closer against the ground, crept as far as possible under the leaves in the hope of escaping all violence. Dark shadows called out to me, striking out. I hoped for a miracle. My body trembled. "Little Lambert, is this now the end for us? Have all our efforts been in vain?"

Isaac then suddenly came to my mind. Isaac, who had prayed for me and had predicted that Lambert and I would survive the bloodshed.

Then there was a loud creaking. Branches hit me in the face. A dark figure emerged suddenly from the shadows and yelled out with triumphant contempt: "Here, here ... two more! Come on out! Stand up! Quickly, filthy cockroaches! Hurry up!" He blew on his whistle. He hit me on my back with his stick. A few of his companions came walking up: "Hey, more snakes?"

My body convulsed. I struggled to stand up. It was over for us!

"Come on, you! Move it!" and pushing us in front of him, he led us out of the forest to a wider road. On the way he raged: "Don't think we'll allow you the chance to get away! We will get all of you. All you slippery snakes and filthy cockroaches, we'll kill you all! Who else is there with you?" He went to hit me. I tried to defend myself. Lambert was struck instead and he began to cry.

I saw more prisoners being driven towards the edge of the forest; some were bleeding. A few Hutu men, many quite young, were standing around, enflamed by the thrill of the hunt. One had blood on his hands and on his machete.

An Interahamwe came over to me. He stamped on my head. He was requesting to see my identity card. "Your card! Show me your card!" One simple word would now condemn me to death: TUTSI. The card? I'd already lost that card to them at a blockade. Confiscated! He stared at me in disbelief. I explained myself by saying that my card had been confiscated by his colleagues at a roadblock.

"You're a Tutsi and you don't want to admit it, you lying bitch. Stand there!" and he pushed me forcefully in the direction of those who shared my destiny.

The pack of merciless killers grew, but with it also the number of prisoners. I saw people vomiting, heard men and women begging for mercy, children crying, appealing to their fathers or mothers for comfort, eyes wide with fear. Some of them panicked, ran away screaming and were brought roughly back again to the desperate group. Even the smallest got a slap. I thought about my own children.

The bastards randomly hit out at anyone for no reason. Only to frighten us, to make us scared. They swore at us, called us every name under the sun just to humiliate us, to belittle us. Together with the rest of their gang, fanatical youths, probably already drunk, they formed a tight circle enclosing us so that no one could get away. Lambert had quietened down again.

When one of the killers felt that there were no more 'snakes' and no more 'cockroaches' to be found and that everyone had been captured, he gave the order to start walking. A long pitiful line of misery set off walking. Men, women and children, crying, desperate. But there were people in our group who were resigned to their fate or people who spoke comforting words to console others. The pathetic wailing procession staggered along the path and out of the forest. The killers accompanied us, marching to the rhythm of their songs, full of hatred and contempt. We left the forest path and came out on a wider road, direction Gatagara. We passed many destroyed houses. Burned out carcasses with destroyed roofs, charred walls and dark doorways that stared at us with hollow, empty looks. Like sad witnesses, they marked the final passage of the countless innocent victims that had passed by there on their way to death, the sorry remnants of where people had once gone about their happy lives.

Slowly we approached the scene of the horror, the Gatagara checkpoint, where people were hanging around and there was a sense of rebellion in the air.

Some distance before the checkpoint, close to the centre of Gatagara, several men directed us all, wildly gesticulating and swearing, towards a wide pit. I noticed that even more Tutsis were being herded in lines, like livestock, in the direction of the pit. I muttered to Lambert that we had reached the end of our flight and that we would see each other again in heaven.

All the prisoners, maybe as many as a hundred and fifty, were now herded together and there was a lot of pushing and pulling. The murderers screamed their orders, swinging their machetes; spectators cheered and swore as if we were criminals. Their foul cheering polluted the air.

In that terrifying atmosphere, so horrifying and inauspicious, nobody felt any chance of escaping their fate. Without mercy we were herded closer towards the pit while the killers walked among us, violently forcing people left and right into the appropriate lines, calling: "Men and boys together. Women and girls together. Sit on the ground!"

Chaos ensued. Distraught parents, brothers and sisters too, all had to look for their own line. A wailing movement started forward: pushing, confusion, emotional goodbyes, clinging arms, the overwhelming fear of death.

This was the end of the road. Children screamed in panic, inconsolably crying; adults shouted, cried, begged. Heartrending images.

Through my tears, however, I saw people speaking words of courage to each other, or to their children, to die bravely. I saw people with their eyes closed, who started softly speaking to themselves, praying and creating a surreal and calm atmosphere around them.

At the edge of the pit the line of men and boys was growing slowly, and a line of women and girls was forming.

My body resisted. Death was looking me in the eye and sneering. Bewildered, afraid, discouraged, I found the women's line and stood almost at the end in the grass. In front of me sat a mother, arms wrapped around her young daughter.

Suddenly, above the sound of everything else, the loud, rough voice of a man called out that we should speak our final words. Again, there was panic. People began to pray, to wail. Children cried and they began to scream and shout in spite of their parents' attempts to calm them.

There are two utterances I will never forget, words spoken by the children to their murderers: "I'll tell my dad! I'll tell my dad! And he'll come after you with his machete." The other was: "Forgive us, we don't want to be Tutsi anymore!"

Since I was almost at the back of the line of women and girls, I went through an unbearable torture: witnessing the atrocious undignified deaths of almost all of the others, in anticipation of my own death. Waiting, resigned, praying; against my better judgement, hoping; in fear and panic, sweating, until it was time for me and Lambert.

All of those condemned to death were eventually directed towards the appropriate place. The tension was charged up to explosive levels.

A small group of men, Interahamwe, in their hated uniform, with their machetes, egged on by the spectators' coarse allusions and humiliating chanting, made their way through the lines of boys and men. At the front of the line, by the sinister gaping pit, the killers dragged the first man to his feet, tore off his clothes and started violently hacking at his body.

The cracking of splintered bones echoed deep in my ears, followed by unearthly screams of agony. Gushing, the blood flowed in dark red streams from the body of the unfortunate victim, thick red drops spattering over the barbaric killers and the first men standing in the line of death. A jolt of shock and horror swept through those waiting. One of the killers inspected the dismembered body and a dull thud followed as he dumped it into the pit.

The next man was seized, and then another. They were undressed and the same bloodthirsty ritual was repeated. They hacked away at the desperately screaming Tutsis as if they were trees. Sinking to the ground, they were then finished off by gleaming metal. If they were still alive, the victim was beaten with sticks or was stoned in order to extinguish any last flicker of life.

Chilling screams, moaning and cries of agony; confused, crying children, and the bloodthirsty triumphant glorification of hatred all melted together in this hell, in this abyss of death.

The atmosphere in the place was indescribable. A suffocating pressure was hanging over this living graveyard. Words like 'terrifying', 'abhorrent', 'gruesome', 'inhuman' cannot even begin to convey the horror of the images that played out before my eyes. The events that took place there no longer fit into our worldview and surpass anything that could possibly be understood by humans. I looked at the ground and prayed, waiting for my turn. There were sometimes victims who were not dead yet. Mutilated, bleeding to death in the pit among the bodies piling up around them, they groaned unintelligible words. I heard them mumble: "Aheza mwijuru", "We shall be joyfully reunited in heaven." Another severely wounded man said the Hail Mary in anticipation of his impending death. I have never been able to rid myself of these extremely gruesome moments.

Blood, blood and even more blood... In the pit, outside of the pit. Red spraying, spattering over the line of those waiting, gushing out of bodies hacked open, over the legs of the killers, the blood formed red puddles on the ground, which was eventually so soaked through that it refused to absorb another drop.

After the liquidation of the men it was time for the boys' line, a job that was soon executed. The murderers hacked up the young bodies without the slightest scruple.

The slaughter continued without delay. The murderers now began to work through the lines of women and girls, unaffected and insensitive to the appalling, indescribable screaming and fearful crying.

All those terrible screams and the dreadful way this depraved atmosphere left its trail have fixed themselves in my head. I cannot bear to hear children crying now: I have to put my fingers in my ears.

The slaughter is slowly reaching its end. I look ahead of me. The pit is filling up with bodies thrown on top of each other.

Lifeless or squirming towards death, begging aloud, groaning, softly praying, helplessly breathing in their final moments, begging to be released from the pain.

Death looks me deep in the eyes. In my line I count three people, three women before me.

In those final moments, Isaac's words occur to me in a flash, I hear his voice once again making his prediction: "You shall not die, your child shall not die, I shall not die, my daughter shall not die either. We shall see each other again in this life when the killing has ended."

And yet look at me sitting here waiting. Death has come so unavoidably close and it has already taken so many people with it. How can I get out of this hell alive? Surrounded by blind hatred, no one has ever managed to escape. It is over! It's the end, Lambert!

In desperation I pray to God to spare me so that I may bear witness to the bloodbath that has taken place here.

Time is running out. I wonder: which of the two of us should go first: Lambert or I? There is a mother sitting in front of me with her young daughter and I summon the courage to ask her: "Which of you will go first, your daughter or you?" The woman turns towards me and answers calmly: "I have accepted that we are both going to die. For me, who goes first is no longer important, it's all over anyway."

Still I wonder whether Lambert or I should go first. But Isaac is convinced that I shall not die. So many confusing thoughts dart through my mind! Consolation, doubts, everything goes through me.

My whole body is trembling, I close my eyes for a moment and then open them again to see if it's my turn yet. I turn my head and look at Lambert to let him know that our flight has come to an end and that death has caught up with us.

I think of my other children, who have hopefully escaped death and have no idea where their mother is about to meet her death. I see Joyeuse and Claudette before me, looking for me, asking if anyone happens to have seen where their mother died. I imagine Germain asking Olivier where they can find their murdered mother. The murderers have finished off another woman from our line.

Impulsively, without thinking, I say a prayer, the prayer of a woman with her child in danger of death: "My almighty God, we are going to die. These murderers say that they first killed You before they killed all the Tutsis. But I, I still believe that there is an immortal God. You are a God who sees, listens and acts. In Your goodness, save at least someone who can relate what has happened here. Let it be me, oh Lord! A great number of Tutsis have already been killed. Heed my prayer! Let it be me! Once saved I shall bear witness to Your strong hand and to You as a living God!"

Bent over, having finished my prayer, I open my eyes and look at the ground. I wait for what is coming. A man comes and stands near me. Is it my turn to die?

"Voilà, la maîtresse!"

On the threshold of death I hear a voice. A voice next to me says: "Voilà, la maîtresse."

La maîtresse, the teacher!

The teacher? The teacher!

Who is that? Who is it that has recognised me?

Total confusion takes hold of me. I raise my head with a jerk. My eyes seek out the voice and see a young man standing next to me. I strain to look, trying to recognise him. Who can that be? It is difficult to make out his face. It is covered with banana leaves. It confuses me. The strangest thoughts shoot through my mind. I am dying. Who is calling: the teacher? Can it be a pupil that was once in my class?

The young man bends over me, takes my arm and I hear him say: "Come with me! Out of the line!" I struggle to my feet, only thinking of death, and I stand there confused, looking at him in the middle of this blood-soaked slaughter. I wait to see what he is going to do with me. He takes me by the arm again and pushes me ahead of him, away from the condemned, groaning grave.

Behind me I hear him say: "Do you remember, in class you always let me borrow your BIC-pen?" It starts to come back to me: Munyaneza, a boy from such a poor family that they couldn't afford to buy him a pen. I had regularly lent him my pen when he was a little boy in my class so that he could copy what I had written on the board.

I heard him say that he would do his absolute best to save me. The murderers were so busy undressing victims and hacking with their machetes, throwing stones at the still-living victims in the pit, that no one noticed what had happened with me. It was not uncommon for a man to take a woman off to rape her before killing her. We were now out of sight of the killers.

"Go! Quickly!" he said softly.

"Go and die somewhere else. I cannot kill you."

And beyond reach of the group of killers, he gave me back my freedom.

I hesitated but then I ran and ran. I ran, still completely obsessed with death. I ran as far away as possible from that terrible pit, from all those desperate, bleeding, dying bodies, bathing in agonising pain.

Run! I had escaped the claws of that monstrous death. Run! Run! It didn't matter where to. Just away from here! My eyes still saw blood everywhere I ran. I was running through the blood, constantly looking back over my shoulder, afraid that someone may be following. But there was no one. No one.

Eventually, I came to a smaller forest where I had already hidden previously. A little further on, I collapsed to the ground and crawled with Lambert under the bushes.

SAVED BY THE BIBLE

Disoriented, like a ball tossed around by fate, I felt myself sinking into madness. Every heartbeat sent death pounding through my body, crippling fear washed over me in waves, certain death and the freedom I had won back battled each other inside my head. I trembled and shook, sighed and moaned, lost all self-control.

And before my eyes ran blood, blood that flowed, that just kept streaming. Whether my eyes were open or shut made no difference. I kept seeing that dripping, spattering blood before me and I could not push it away.

From deep within me came the realization that I was still alive. That I lay safe here for the moment. But inside, I also began to wrestle with the question: Should I be happy with my escape? With the freedom I had gotten back?

At a certain point I became aware of little Lambert on my back. He was gripping his little eyes tightly closed. Not until four days later would he open them.

I stayed there with him in that little forest for a week, hiding from the gruesome, murderous outside world that had almost made me into its victim and of which I was now a witness in such an extreme way.

During those days all sorts of things ran through my head: Why did I not accept death along with the others? Why didn't I want that? I would be dead now! What is my life worth anymore? Can there still be a normal life for me?

Doubt and wry, sick thoughts held me fast. Disorientation and confusion took control of my body.

At the end of the week, when I was slowly beginning to get control of myself again and the fear ebbed away a little, I was awakened by sounds of shouting and singing, like the voices of hunters pursuing game. This time, it was a group of men accompanied by dogs, dogs that were searching every inch of the woods for fugitives. Every Tutsi they found was killed immediately.

"Won't it ever stop?" I groaned dispiritedly and crawled farther away.

It didn't help much. Peering through the grass I saw a dog run sniffing over the ground not far from us, now here, now there. He stood still for a moment, looked up, and then put his nose to the ground again. But now he was coming towards my thicket and he started to search thoroughly. He wormed his way towards me through the leaves and branches and his short, excited snout came nearer and nearer. The beast stopped for a moment, looked searchingly in my direction, pricked up his ears and crept cautiously towards us. My breath faltered. In just a moment his bark would show the men where we were. Frightened, I crept still further away. My body scraped over something hard in my clothes. I felt for it and realized that it was a book. Isaac's Bible! I pulled it carefully out, took it in my right hand, waited until the dog was standing right in front of me, and then used the Bible to give him a firm blow on the nose. The animal recoiled, let out a little squeak and backed off, but without barking. He trotted back to his boss, who glanced quickly our way but must have thought his dog had seen a little animal in the thickets.

The tension, that had become almost unbearable, exploded in my body and then flowed slowly away. Once again I had escaped death, but I felt that I could not continue this life for long.

The murderous band slowly left the place where we were, but in next to no time they had carried out a terrific massacre. They killed even more people than on the day of the pit in Gatagara. People hiding by the river, people huddled in fields, even people in trees. The whole area was combed through with dogs. By the use of these animals hundreds of Tutsis were killed that day, butchered by merciless murders.

I stayed hidden in that forest for a short time. It was familiar to me because it was close to our house.

But the emotions of the last few days caused a crisis in my little Lambert. He moaned and began to scream louder and louder, "Papa! Papa! And I also heard sounds that resembled the names of his sisters and brothers. I was astonished and dismayed because it was the first time I had heard him say anything.

His howling drove me to despair. "Lambert, please. Softly! Be quiet!" Lambert cried harder: "Papa! Papa!" I saw that his crying would put our lives in danger so I tried to calm him, but nothing helped. Until he began to drool and a big lump of mucous worked its way up, getting stuck in his throat and mouth. I tried to get that accumulated slime out of his mouth with my fingers but was unsuccessful. But it had to come out quickly! What had an older woman told me once? "When someone is dying, he throws up yellow mucous!" That was where I was now. I had to seek help. But who could I still trust if I went to ask? In despair, I bound Lambert on my back again and decided to run to one of our neighbours to whom we had given a cow now and then, and one of whose sons was our godchild.

I had not gone two steps before Isaac's Bible fell to the ground. I picked it up, but it was now no more than ballast. I threw it in the bushes with the idea that, if I survived, I would go back and find it. I turned around to see where the Bible had landed and... I couldn't believe my eyes. Ripe strawberries were growing on that spot! I did not hesitate a moment but picked them and used the juice to clean Lambert's mouth, and now I was able to remove that great clump of mucous. I squeezed the juice from more strawberries and gave it to him to drink. Slowly his eyes closed and he looked lifeless. Only a little tic, a vein in his throat, showed that he was alive. I saw that his situation was very critical. His legs stiffened, he clamped down his teeth on his lower lip, and then he went limp. His tongue now hung out of his mouth. Everything suggested that he was in the middle of a deathly struggle.

In desperation, I laid him carefully on the ground again and gave him more strawberry juice to drink. He slept and slept and slept. I was between fear and hope that he would make it, and kept regularly pouring strawberry juice in his mouth to help him survive. He did not wake up until three days later. You could see it as a resurrection. I still compare it with the Bible story of Lazarus.

After I was convinced that the worst was behind us with Lambert, I started out again. First I wandered around for a while, telling myself I would try to find refuge with Eliyer Gakumba, who had once received a cow from us. But walking was difficult. My legs were very weak and I felt lifeless. I was going too slow and I also had to keep my wits about me to make sure that everything was safe.

Uncomfortably, painfully, feeling helpless, I sought my way. I came across a young man holding a 'clou', a club with nails, in his hands. Without saying anything, he unexpectedly gave me a blow on my neck and I fell over. He really wanted to hit Lambert, but the child escaped the blow by bending just in time and the club landed on my head.

That wild idiot kept going, whacking and thumping my legs without saying a word. My legs still have great black scars from the blows of that 'clou'.

Finally the damned lout did say something. "If you survive, these blows with the club will leave marks on your body and make it hard for you to ever walk well again." And he added sarcastically "I dropped behind my group to deal with you, you dirty cockroach!" Then he walked away to get back to his companions. I asked myself: How can this rascal know that I am a Tutsi?

I felt my body glowing and my legs burning so painfully. At first I was not able to stand but I finally made it, although with difficulty. I massaged my legs and so was able to stay upright. I plucked up all my strength and staggered out to find the house of Eliyer Gakumba.

On the way I began to rave. Voices in my head screamed: "Stop her, she's going to escape, that woman with the child on her back! Kill her! Hutu-power, Hutu-power!"

The cries were unbelievably loud in my head, the result of everything I had endured in the last few weeks.

HIDING AT OUR GODSON'S

Finally, half-stumbling from exhaustion, I reached Eliyer's house and knocked on the door. No one opened it. But I heard his voice from behind the door:
- "Who's there?"
- "Beata."
- "Beata who?"
- "Beata! Placide's wife!"
- "Which Placide?"
What was this all about? What was the purpose of all these questions? He knew me.
- "Placide from Remera!"
- "Who is standing with you at my door?"
- "I am with my youngest child."
- "Where is Placide?"
- "He may be dead; I heard he was."
- "Who told you that?"
- "I don't know exactly who told me any more."
- "Where is the gun that he owned?"
- "He didn't own a gun, that's pure slander!!"
Who told him those lies? Gun! We had never had a weapon in our house. There was a tense, unfriendly atmosphere at the door. And why wouldn't he open up?
- "Do you have that gun with you?"

- "What? No, of course not! How could we have gotten a gun? No really, we never had a gun in our house!"
- "What do you want from the house of a Hutu?"
- "I came to ask for a place to hide. If you don't want to give me that, then please just kill me and bury me. Give me a real grave so I won't be eaten by crows and other wild animals. I've run up and down the hills for long enough. And if you hide me, I will consider it a sign of your gratitude for what our family has done for you."
- "So you want to make me pay for that cow? To put me down and humiliate me? Take all four of our cows!"
- "Have you forgotten that we had a whole herd?"
- "And take the bicycle you gave me, too! And ride away on it, I don't care where!"

During this whole unfriendly - I might even say hateful - exchange of words, the door remained closed. I was outside, hopeless and tired, and he was inside. So inhospitable. If someone knocks on your door, you don't make him stand there, you invite him into the house.

But his son Emmanuël, who had been our godson for more than twenty-five years, grew curious and opened the door suddenly, which meant I could get into the room. There were a lot of people at home, and I even saw little children in the room.

What surprised and disappointed me terribly was that no one greeted me. They all knew me well; we regarded each other as friends and we used to visit each other often. We were very easy together, almost like family. But now? No one said a word to me. Silence. A chilly, tense atmosphere greeted me.

Emmanuël broke the hostile silence and suggested I should hide in the ceiling somewhere in the house, where my attackers would not find me. These ruthless people, murderers really, used to gather regularly at his father's house because he was in charge of the nearby barricade. Emmanuël insisted that his father had to hide me as a sign of gratitude for all the good things that their family had received from us. He even warned his father: if he dared to kill me, then it might happen that he - Emmanuël that is - might do something to his father.

Then his younger brother Fidèle came in, making a great racket. He had just returned from a killing spree. He ignored me at first. He told in an excited voice about the important part he had played in a massacre he had participated in: of a whole lot of "dirty Tutsis" that they finished off as they were sitting down to eat a meal. The Tutsis had prepared the meal in a banana plantation and he described the slaughter in great detail. Everyone laughed and chuckled, to which he reacted: "It's really true! Their children are serpents, because if you mistreat them they don't even let out a peep. I've seen it myself now."

At the same time he showed us the clothes he had taken from the bodies of the victims and gave them to the children to try on. He was also carrying a full bag of meat with him.

He named the people they had thrown half dead into a pit and even, with unbelievable sadism, mentioned the names of victims that had begged him for water in their death throes. So he boasted of his deeds. Proudly he elaborated on their extreme abuse, on their rapes of Tutsi women and girls. His jacket and machete were covered with blood, an unmistakable illustration of his devilish stories.

After all his bluster he threw a stack of identity cards from his victims on the ground. I bent over a little to see if there were any cards of people I knew. He called, "Hey, are you going to make trouble! You want to show us you can read! Just wait a little! I'm going to freshen up, because I've earned it, and then I'm going to occupy myself with you. Not a single Tutsi can remain alive! We're rooting you out! Our descendents will ask: What did Tutsis look like?'"

After these words he grabbed a large machete, smeared with the blood of murdered Tutsis. He didn't even feel he needed to clean it, but began to cut the meat from the bag into pieces, throwing it in the pan. His sister lit the fire to bake the meat, but she didn't think it was necessary to clean the cooking gear or the pans, either. This to me was clear proof that the killers had become animals.

I returned from my thoughts because our godson once again made it clear to everyone that he suggested I should go and hide in the ceiling somewhere in the house. He took me with him to a side room and pointed to the ceiling. I crept up and noticed that it was made of reeds woven together. Between the woven reeds you could see who was below, but you could also see outside.

I prayed to God that I would not sink through that thin ceiling. But a lot of bad luck sometimes brings a little good luck with it. All the misery of the last few weeks had caused me to lose a lot of weight. Now I weighed only forty kilos and Lambert weighed only five. One problem was the searing pain I still felt in my hips and thighs from that miserable rascal's blows with the club, so I had a hard time lying on one of my hips. Luckily my guardian angel Emmanuël took good care of us. He brought us guava fruit, mostly to keep Lambert quiet because if he started crying he could betray our hiding place.

After an anxious night my health grew worse, and over the course of the day it became critical. I was almost out of my mind, hardly breathing any more, suffering from a terrible headache. When Emmanuël saw me in that wretched state, he sighed. "If you people could only die without being hacked to pieces by those bloodthirsty killers. If only that was possible." He began to cry and went away. Within ten minutes he came back and gave me pills in the hope that they would cure my headache. I was still well enough to want to know what kind of pills they were and he answered in an indignant tone: "Do you doubt me because I'm not a doctor? Sometimes Tutsis act like little children. Take these pills and if they make you better, that's good! If they kill you, then you belong with the Tutsis who are already dead!"

I put the pills in my hand and saw that they were chlorenphenicol, which I knew of. I asked for water to take them with. "Don't you have any spit?" he asked shortly. "How can you have any spit if your mouth is completely dry?" I answered. He couldn't give me any water. But after he left, I suddenly remembered that he had brought me guavas. I could chew the fruit and swallow the pills along with the juice.

I had barely taken the pills when a dull, rhythmic thumping from outside reverberated from the ground to the ceiling. A group of savage men came near us stomping and singing. They amused themselves with inflammatory, filthy, insulting songs. This noisy, disorderly gang, full of hatred and contempt for Tutsis, gathered for a meeting at the door, undoubtedly in order to lay their murderous, satanic plans. They came inside noisily, talking loudly together and drinking banana beer. I heard a couple of them bragging about the large number of victims they had already killed. Some had not killed anyone but had hunted out fugitives for others to kill, without having to themselves hack Tutsis with their machetes. But I also heard people saying, "What we do here, eating, drinking, killing Tutsis, will not be without consequences." Their deeds would not go unpunished, someone said. In the group, there was some uneasiness about what the consequences might be and what that would mean for them.

The beer was all gone, the gathering was over. They decided to go on with the Tutsi hunt in the grass fields of Gatagara where I had hidden for a few days. Then they left.

After two days the hideous shouting sounded again: "Oo-oo-oo! Oo-oo-oo! Oo-oo-oo!!" The same people were coming back home very early, still shouting and yelling.

"Yes!" called one, "the work pays twice as much when it's done early in the day!"

By 'work' and 'working' those people simply meant murdering. 'Going to work' meant setting off to kill Tutsis.

With cries of "Oo-oo-oo", they came inside yelling, "There's a Tutsi here! There must be a Tutsi here!!" They began searching the rooms, looking under and between all the objects, between the piled-up straw mats where the beans lay. One of them came into the room where I was lying in the ceiling. He reacted impulsively, as if bitten by a bee: "I'm a specialist in smelling out Tutsis. I smell one! That can't be wrong! I never make a mistake!" He looked everywhere and I was afraid that the shifty son Fidèle or his mother might have told this man secretly about my presence. I didn't trust that Fidèle at all. He seemed to be an inhuman, brutish murderer. "I'll eat you up tomorrow!" he had threatened once, when he found me down in the house by chance.

He had probably murdered many children in a grisly way, driving a knife deep in their bodies and carving out their hearts with a single movement, so that their screams were quickly silenced.

The searching Hutu pointed his spear at the ceiling and began thrusting. Now here, now there. "Where is the Tutsi? Where is that serpent?" It is very likely that someone had spoken of me and my hiding place and this man knew of it. It would not have surprised me at all, because the night before, Eliyer had held a family council to discuss the question of how quickly they could get me out of the house. But Emmanuël had advised his family members to save me, saying that if I stayed alive they could make money showing me as a sort of tourist attraction. I would be a curiosity, the only Tutsi left.

At a certain point the lout poking at the ceiling with his spear noticed that there was blood on the point when he pulled it out. I felt pain in one of my thighs and when I passed my hand over that spot, I saw blood on it. He had pricked me. I heard him shouting, "There, see? I never make a mistake! My strong nose sniffs out all the Tutsis!" He had discovered me! For a few seconds my mind scrambled around looking for a solution. My money! I had taken a considerable sum with me when I left the house. In spite of everything that had happened, I still had that money with me, safe and dry. Could that save me? I had no choice! I had to decide quickly.

I climbed down at once. He looked surprised when I walked softly toward him. I whispered in his ear: "What do you need my blood for? Spare me!" and I gave him 5,000 Rwandan francs, money I was carrying knotted in my outer garment. How would he react? Luckily, he did not refuse my offer. He whispered back "Quiet! Quiet! This is between us. If the others hear about it, they'll rush me and take the money. Go back!" Relieved, I went back to my hiding place in the ceiling. Once again, providence was on my side.

The man with the spear ordered everyone out again, saying there weren't any Tutsis to be found in the house. Outside he blew his whistle as a sign to leave.

After their noisy departure I left Lambert up there, sleeping in our hiding place, and climbed down. I went to the banana plantation to search for a plant, 'inyabarasanya', that we used to use to heal wounds when we were young.

As I searched I could hear the killers' rowdy yelling and singing from all sides. The frightening noise grew louder and came dangerously close by. What now? I didn't dare to go back! I ducked quickly into a hut that stood nearby. It seemed to be a mill for grinding sorghum into meal with stones. If they found me here, I could pretend to be a Hutu.

I began to grind grain. I heard the killers searching everywhere with their usual racket. One or two of them saw me in the hut, busy grinding. One asked if I was a Tutsi. I was afraid for my life, but I had to look unconcerned and keep grinding. I mumbled an answer: "If I were a Tutsi, would I still be alive? Don't bother me because I'm making yeast meal for banana beer and I'm almost finished. You'd better come back when the beer is ready."

"Yes, save some for us! Don't sell it all!" The leader of the gang ordered everyone to leave and to come back in two days, when the beer was ready.

As soon as they were gone, I hastily went to the house to hide in the ceiling again, but I was held back by an angry Eliyer.

"Take your child with you and disappear!" he said in a gruff voice. I was confused. I begged him to let me stay there, but his wife and even his children stood by him and called out meanly, angrily "No! Away with you! Out! On the street!!"

My thoughts in a tumult, I climbed up to get Lambert and left. Where to? I had no idea.

All I could do was walk back up the hill. I came to a little trading center called 'Cercle'. This center was famous as a place where Interahamwe militias could get proper, serious training to be skilled militia.

There were people to the left and right of the barricade. My eyes fell on an area where a goat was being cut into pieces. A little farther up sat a man and a girl, but I quickly saw that they were being forced to stay sitting on the ground. The man explained to the militias that he came from the commune of Gikongoro and had fled from one hiding place to another with his daughter. Everyone in his group had been killed on their way to Burundi, except for him and his daughter. He had hardly finished speaking when one of the Interahamwe raised his machete and gave him a blow on the neck. The blood shot up like a fountain and streamed down his back in rivers to the loose red sand. His head hung down, dangling halfway down his trunk. The man slumped farther forward. Another killer gave him a last blow on the head with his machete. Dying, my fellow sufferer murmured almost inaudibly, "Lord have mercy on me." The girl turned her head away in shock, but spoke immediately, without any fear in her voice: "Kill me too! I am not worth more than my father, my mother, my brothers and sisters, my friends and everyone else who was murdered."

I will never forget what happened next. My memory will never be clear of the shocking images of the gruesome, nauseating and cruel slaughter of that girl. The thugs flung themselves on the brave child all at the same time like wild beasts and hit and hacked her with their machetes, battered and beat her with nail-studded clubs. Those ravening beasts literally hacked her to bits. "I am innocent" were her last words. What had once been a beautiful human body, what was once a girl, beloved by family and friends, had become a formless, maimed, unrecognizable mass, a pile of meat. "I am innocent!"

After that inhuman frenzy one of the genocidaires thrust his machete, still dripping with blood, under my nose. "Who are you really?" I said nothing but stepped forward, giving him an almost imperceptible sign, and he followed me. Because of this, the people in the trading center thought that we belonged together. A little farther on, out of their sight, I untied the knot of my shawl, my kanga, and took out my last bit of money, 10,000 Rwandan francs. I offered it to him secretly. I made it clear that I had to get past in peace.

"Another bit of food is being offered to me!" he said loudly to himself. He waved to me to go.

Afraid, not knowing where I was going, I hesitated. I was in a deplorable state. I felt empty and miserable. "Ayii!", what a situation! I was also thinking about all those victims, about the father and his daughter. "Ayii!" Dark feelings overcame me. I was finished. I could only express my despair in sighing and moaning, only "Ayii!", nothing but "Ayii!" Those terrible murders.

LONGING FOR DEATH

My despair led to disorientation and morbid thoughts. I could see only one way out: to go to the house of Esron Mutabaruka, leader of the Interahamwe and president of the MRND Hutu party of the Kigoma commune. I knew that Esron Mutabaruka had guns in his house. I knew his wife Venantie well; she was a teacher like me. I wanted to ask her if Esron would shoot me dead. Exhaustion and not knowing what to do had driven me to the brink of the abyss, to the edge of despair and I saw death as the only solution for my hopeless existence.

That desperate thought led me to an open asphalt road that offered no chance at all of hiding. Without the protection of banana plantations and forests, without cover from tall crops in fields, I went my way. I no longer cared who saw us walking.

The heat now had a crippling effect, and sweat covered my whole body. Weakened, tired, I stumbled here and there over the hot, hard road.

When I had dragged myself along for a while, I came to a stall selling banana beer. The owner stood talking with some customers and giving them beer. One of the customers who sat there drinking called out suddenly: "Hey, what do I see now? A Tutsi!"

Another looked surprised and reacted dumbfoundedly: "Are there still Tutsis alive? That's bold! Walking around in broad daylight!"

One of them jumped up immediately, came over to me and began to ask questions:

- "Where are you going?"
- "To Mutabaruka," I answered in a tired, hoarse voice.
- "What are you going to do there?"
- "I'm going to visit family; now let me pass."
- "Where do you come from?"
- "From Gatagara." I looked at the man impatiently.
- "From Gatagara. From which family, then?" The poor victims of the mass murder came to my mind.
- "Please don't ask me too much; I've lost everything. I don't have anything anymore. I don't know anything anymore."
"Oh, no? I'll refresh your memory."
His machete lay next to him. He took the great knife and waved it back and forth under my nose. Then he let the weapon fall.
"See you soon!" he said mockingly.
I got out of there as quickly as possible, in spite of my battered body and heavy heart, because I was deathly afraid of being killed with a machete.
In that despair I kept trying to get to the house of Esron Mutabaruka. A little farther along, a soldier was patrolling on the other side of the road. All by himself. He carried a gun and I was sure he would stop me and shoot me. To be shot dead; that was a thought I had reconciled myself to.
"Lambert, if this is our end, it seems to me to be better to die from a bullet than from a machete." I waited anxiously for the soldier's reaction. He glanced at me for a moment but did not try to hold me back, let alone shoot me dead. No, he just kept walking, did not stretch his hand out towards me, so I walked past him towards Esron Mutabaruka to meet my death.
The long walk took much of my last strength, but finally I got to the house. A door led into an enclosure where women were busily shelling peas. They turned, and searching, even suspicious, eyes examined me.
"Muraho", "Good day."
Some returned my greeting. Others said nothing but began murmuring to each other. Finally one of them asked:
"Are you looking for someone?"

"Well, I would like to speak to Venantie, or her husband," I somehow answered loudly.

Venantie, who was inside, heard her name and came out quickly. Surprised, she cried, "Oh now, look! Beata, she's still alive!" She took my hand and drew me towards her. "How happy I am to see you!" Venantie held me even more firmly. "Come inside." I followed her and went into the living room where her husband and two daughters were sitting.

Mutabaruka seemed to be really unpleasantly surprised when I came into the room. "Am I seeing right? Is the wife of Placide standing before me? Declared dead in Gatagara?" Of course he meant that day when my former student saved me.

Angrily, Mutabaruka pushed his chair back. He went to a cupboard and, groaning, picked up a thick register and began to look hastily through it, checking to see who had a cross next to his name and who did not. That was supposed to indicate whether or not that person had been killed (yet). His face twisted when his eyes fell on my name. Angrily, raging, he slammed his fist on the table and swore: "That damned son of Bruno lied to me. He'll regret this! He expressly informed me that she was dead!" I answered him: "Really I'm dead already, it's just that there's still a little bit of air left in my body, holding me up. My body is finished." But his wife, who had watched everything from close by, pushed me quickly out the door and led me to another room.

"Wait here!" A little later she came back with a bottle of juice and a cup of milk. She offered me the juice and gave Lambert the milk. At the same moment her husband burst out in another fit of rage. The reason for his rage soon became clear to me when Venantie told me her husband had just received a report that the Inkotanyi - the liberation army of the RPF - had already taken Bugesera and the river Mayaga had already been crossed. If the Rwandan army, the FAR, had not destroyed the bridge, then the Inkotanyi had probably been successful in occupying the area and saving many Tutsis in the south of the country. Now that he had more serious affairs on his mind, Mutabaruka had already forgotten about me.

Venantie stayed with me and Lambert and asked where I had been all this time. I told her about my wanderings, our life in the woods, the shocks and dangers I had survived, and that I saw the protective hand of God in it because it was a miracle I was still alive. I also told her that my despair, which had driven me to wish for death, had brought me to her house. But Venantie encouraged me to keep on, to keep praying, because there was more and more of a chance that I might escape the deadly attacks. A growing chance existed that the RPF would quickly put an end to the massacres.

In the meantime she led me to yet another room that had a mattress in it and suggested that I lie there with Lambert to recover from all the horrible things we had been through. She even gave me the key, so that I could lock the door and not let anyone in. And she brought a big tin, in which Lambert could do his business.

Within a quarter of an hour I already felt somewhat better. We could stay here relatively safely, out of the rain and storm, far from the bushes. It was also wonderful to be able to lie full-length on the mattress and hide in a room with a lock.

But I couldn't sleep. I kept hearing the panicked screams, the frightened and helpless voices of the people hounded to their deaths. I kept hearing the frightful singing of the Interahamwe, their threatening gunshots. Everything flowed together in a mixture of terrible, inexplicable sounds, so frightening and insistent that I could hardly suppress the urge to scream. The most horrible nightmares played in my head like a film. Until, at a certain moment, the bad dreams fell away a little and I became calmer inside and was able to close my eyes for a short time.

Suddenly I heard screaming again and at first I thought it was in my head, caused by the terrible dreams that still tormented me. I heard fierce voices calling:

"Was he killed?"

"Yes, he is dead."

"Who killed him? That person has the right to a reward!"

"Everyone! Everyone helped. We took turns bashing him with our machetes! We did good work."

I stood up and crept very carefully to the window so I could listen better. My frightened suspicion that they were coming my way was confirmed by a voice coming from the other side of my locked door, whispering: "Don't make a sound, be quiet; don't open the door and make sure your child is also silent!" Venantie's voice warned me against the violence. Keep Lambert quiet? My brave boy was so upset, so exhausted that he didn't want to cry any more. So he couldn't cause me problems.

After her warning, Venantie quickly left the house. Outside in the courtyard, I heard one of the people ask her suspiciously: "Is that serpent here?" There was a short silence, but then Venantie lashed out at him: "Here? How can you suggest that someone would be here? Where did you get that ridiculous idea?" She turned angrily to the group: "Who did you come here for? Who did you kill?"

Someone from the group reacted: "We discovered an old man hiding in an avocado tree."

"Which old man, precisely?"

"A little old man from Nyanza. He had been sitting in the avocado tree for some time, living off the fruits."

He added in another tone, suddenly sounding worried: "The RPF has already reached Busoro. We must search quickly; otherwise I'm afraid there will still be Tutsis left and they will give evidence against us. Undoubtedly they'll reveal our deeds." But someone began to sing and other voices joined in immediately. Once again I heard those raw, nauseating songs about their greatest deeds: "Hutus in power, not a single Tutsi will survive, we have killed the children, we have slaughtered the young girls and boys, we have dismembered the men and raped the women, we have killed the old people, we haven't even forgotten the crazy ones."

When they began to sing those songs, I thought immediately of my children and asked myself gloomily whether they, like me, were hidden safe somewhere, or if they were already dead. At that last thought I felt dizzy and nauseous. I quickly grabbed the tin and vomited into it. All the juice came up and, even after everything was out, I kept heaving. It was so intense that it seemed as if my heart would emerge, along with my stomach. I felt totally empty!

The killers, none the wiser from Venantie's answer, went back quickly to search every corner of the enclosure, but not the main dwelling because that was where the great chief lived. They combed through the banana plantation and scoured the whole soy field. In spite of their meticulous search, they looked right over the head of a young man and did not even find the man hiding in a little hut, because Venantie had stuffed him under the braided reed mats that were used to dry grain.

After the genocide I met those two men again at the gacaca. They appeared before the people's court as witnesses for Venantie.

THE RPF APPROACHES

Peace returned in and around the house and, dead tired, I eventually fell asleep. Venantie woke me and told me that the soldiers and supporters of the FAR had prepared to withdraw or flee because of the rapid advance of the RPF. For my own safety she advised me to leave the house the next day and hide in the woods. A new stream of refugees had set out, now involving large groups of Hutus. A number of them would probably come to her husband for refuge, because he was one of the most important leaders of the MRND. It was possible that this could pose a direct threat to me. I spent the last night at Venantie's house in a state of great tension, and slept very badly. The following morning deteriorated into complete chaos. There were loud bangs from all sides; an unbelievable noise from ear-piercing shots. Gunfire, thundering and echoing; bullets whistling in all directions, rapidly shattering objects or hitting the sand. Add to that the shouting and screaming of desperate people running around, fleeing, not knowing what to do - all this created a surreal atmosphere, so terrifying we feared for our lives. Buses of FAR soldiers and their Hutu families drove back and forth, stopping and letting people on and off, on their way to Congo, where they thought they would be safe.

Venantie hurried to my room and urged me to flee with her, but I refused. In her company I would be swept along by the large stream of Hutu refugees, running the risk of being killed by one of them. When she understood that I really did not want to go with her, she took me to the garden and pointed to the chicken coop which might serve as a possible hiding place for me and Lambert. It was an emotional parting, and with the fervent wish that we would see one another again with God's help, we said goodbye and I watched her go.

The chicken coop did not look particularly attractive and it seemed better to me for our safety to leave quickly. With Lambert on my back I walked through the little gate of the banana plantation and found myself back in the midst of the noise of a crowded street. Crying children, bleating goats, lowing cows, shouting people, Hutus from Mayaga on the run, bent under heavy loads, as they were dragging as many things from their houses with them as possible: mattresses, large, heavy bags, baskets and so on. An enormous flood of people poured across the street, often taking up its entire width.

I tried to make my way against the broad stream and all these people were in such a hurry that I did not even stand out as a Tutsi. I realised I had nothing with me. They were heavily laden and asked me in surprise why I wasn't carrying any baggage. Why had I left my things at home? I decided it was best to say nothing in reply and walked on to a house where I knew a woman well.

In order to find out how the inhabitants were, I entered and freed myself of the turbulent crowd. Those whom I encountered in the house were dumbfounded to see me alive. Two older women, Agnes, a member of my husband's family, and Virginie, her neighbour, had also found shelter in the house. Agnes was in tears when she saw me and anxiously asked where Placide was. And my children? Did I know about my children?

I told her I did not know much. I had heard rumours that Placide was no longer alive. As for the fate of my children, I had no idea. During this reunion a man hurried into the house, apparently a Hutu, as we heard him in another room asking, "Are there still cockroaches here?" Jozef, the house owner, insisted that he had not seen a single cockroach, but despite this denial, the man was unconvinced, so he started searching the kitchen, then entered the stable. His search revealed nothing and when leaving the house he urged Jozef to be vigilant and keep an eye on everything and everyone, as not a single Tutsi could be allowed to escape. This Hutu belonged to a group of militia who were unable to forgo searching for Tutsis even on their flight to Congo. At the slightest suspicion they threw their belongings aside and forced their way into houses. Shortly after the departure of the Hutu we heard a loud voice outside screaming commands and an angry movement started up on the road. More houses were searched and the teams then returned, restored their loose baggage to manageable loads again, and the whole lot set off hastily and chaotically, heavily laden, to flee to Congo, where it was safe for them.

Agnes and Virginie felt that it was safer to leave with the turbulent crowd to avoid possible gunfights, but I refused. They set off in the direction of Kabagali, the area where they were born. We parted in tears. It was the last time we were to speak, as I never saw them again. They died, but I do not know how or where.

With Lambert, I had to go in the opposite direction, running against the great current of people. But in the middle of the disordered noise of departing refugees and the loud, booming patter of automatic weapons reverberating among the hills, I felt so restless that I crept into a pit of sawdust to wait until things calmed down.

After a short while, the hill was deserted and only when I was sure I could no longer hear voices did I creep out of the pit and dare to lie in the sun and dry off with Lambert beside me, as we were very wet from the damp sawdust.

I had been lying there a while, eyes closed, when a voice calmly but firmly demanded my attention.

"Hey, you there!"

I turned and saw two soldiers looking suspiciously in our direction. They were speaking Swahili and coming in my direction. One asked me to stand up, which I did with difficulty. I tied Lambert onto my back again. The other soldier asked me curiously why I had not fled like the others.

"I need to go in the other direction to get to my village," I replied nervously. They looked at me intently and I had an uneasy feeling.

"If you are murderers then kill me! If you are liberators then save me! I don't care either way; I have had more than enough of the life I'm leading now!"

One of them grabbed my arm and said, "Calm down! You're not going to die. We are RPF members. We are not killing anyone; we are saving people."

My mouth fell wide open. I couldn't believe my eyes. Here before me stood soldiers from the liberating army. Did this mean the end of the massacres? Was it safe in our country again? A mixture of joy and relief, doubt and sorrow, overcame me. I felt emotional confusion. My body, accustomed to serve as prey for hunting gangs, might have been freed of the primal fear, but could not shake off the pressure of the past difficult months.

The rising happy mood interestingly caused some conflict inside me. I said accusingly, "You are too late, practically all the men have been wiped out and you are at serious risk of being killed yourselves. The Hutus are more savage and cruel than animals. They will devour you like wild beasts, that's how they operate!"

The two soldiers tried to put me at ease. One took Lambert from me and asked me to walk up the hill with him, as a camp had been set up there. Their commander was also there with more soldiers.

The first thing I saw was a young man, extremely restless, with great fear in his eyes, having just escaped from his murderous pursuers, sitting on the ground, safe among the soldiers. My protectors took me to the commander. He wanted to know where I came from. I replied as well as I was able to. But in my anxiety over all the terrible events I had witnessed, as well as my realization of liberation from deadly threat, I was overcome and I asked him not to demand too much of me. I asked him to leave me in peace, as my head was spinning. In a blur I saw images of screaming people, their throats cut, and crying children before me. The most horrific scenes surfaced, and I broke out in a fearful sweat at the memories of those dreadful moments I had been through with others or with Lambert.

The commander respected my request and directed me to a

spot where I could rest. At that moment the young man who had escaped the murderers began to scream: "They are coming, they are there! They are going to kill me! God! Help, here they come…" He kept on shouting, "They are going to kill me! They are coming!" Completely deranged, looking around him wildly, he screamed, "No! No, I am not a Tutsi, believe me! I am not a Tutsi!!" RPF soldiers ran over to him and tried to calm him.

Other soldiers were ordered to go on patrol and track down Tutsis who were still in hiding, to bring them to the safe camp.

The security offered by these soldiers, the warmth they demonstrated, the sympathy they expressed, the comfort they gave us as people who had escaped the murderous claws of the Interahamwe, will remain with me forever.

Shortly afterwards I saw other survivors surface. Among them was Laetitia, a friend and teaching colleague I knew well. I ran straight over to her. She looked at me, incredulous and happy, and we fell crying into one another's arms. After the initial greetings I wanted to know:

"Where are your children?" Her face fell, her eyes filled with tears. "The children! The children! YOH! YOH! My children are all dead! Oh, Beata, I am afraid that your children may no longer be alive either! YOH!"

I had lived for a long time between hope and fear, and my fears were increasingly confirmed. The bad news filled me with great sorrow. Our emotions prevented us from saying everything we had to say. Time and again we came back to our children, our hearts filled and we tried to find out from one another whether one of us could say more about her nearest and dearest than the other. Laetitia hoped I might be able to say more about my children, but I had to admit that I had not received any news at all about them, as I had lost all contact with family and friends during my months of trying to survive.

During our conversation, RPF soldiers came to tell us that they would accompany us all to the 'Centre de Mugandamure', an Islamic centre to which other survivors had been taken. There I met a man called Nsengiyumva who recognised me. He introduced himself as a friend of my husband Placide and invited me to his house in 'Centre de Mugandamure'.

For the moment I could stay with Nsengiyumva. His two sisters, who like their brother had survived the genocide, were also staying there. Our grief over the loss of family members and others close to us was such a heavy load that we cried day and night and sought comfort in one another. I had the hospitality of this family to thank for the fact that I did not have to sleep in overcrowded schools or other buildings, like so many other refugees.

IN SEARCH OF HAPPINESS LOST

In the week that I stayed with Nsengiyumva, I was overcome by the strong desire to go and look at my home. Who would I see there? Had much been destroyed? What was still left for me there?

I decided to ask a soldier from the RPF to accompany me home, but he refused my request. He was unable to guarantee my safety due to the fact that, in various places along the way, there was still fighting going on between the liberating army and the Interahamwe. I was disappointed, but my desire to go home was so great that I wasn't prepared to give up quite so easily.

Two days later I accosted another soldier and tried to convince him to take me with him. This time I had more luck and he agreed. I left Lambert with Nsengiyumva and his sisters, and together we set off on our way. I was desperately hoping to get more information about the fate of my children.

On the way we discussed the events of the previous months and everything that had happened to us. Full of emotion, I told the soldier about the horrific murders committed by the Hutus and the unimaginable fact that some had not even shrunk from killing their grandchildren, parents-in-law, nephews and nieces, aunts and uncles.

On the road back to my house we were confronted in a sinister way by many silent witnesses of the genocide. We saw countless dead bodies, some half buried, some partially dug up, but also many bodies just lying all over the place, along the side of the road. They had been dumped on the roadside, mutilated in the most horrific ways, already severely eaten away by all-consuming death.

The life had literally been beaten out of the bodies of these people. Others, mortally wounded, had been thrown into a pit and this immoral crime had then been hastily and sloppily covered over by a thin layer of red earth.

The dead were not even allowed to rest in peace. Dozens of growling dogs had dug up the lifeless victims with a voracious greed. These savage animals dragged away whole bodies or body parts in their teeth. They drew irregular lines in the sand, forming peculiar images, and so deprived the dead of what little dignity remained. Whole packs of dogs roamed the hills and made the most of the human flesh. This gruesome scene shocked us so much that we continued our journey in silence.

I arrived home. Or rather, what had once been my home and where I had once felt so happy. All the buildings, even where I had lived with my family, had been completely destroyed. All our fields, once fertile fields, had been completely looted. Everything had been taken: bananas, cassava, carrots, potatoes, fruits like 'coeurs de boeuf' tomatoes and guava, which grew around the house. Trees empty, fields bare, the ground gaping open and a lot of pulled-up vegetables. I was completely gutted and as I walked around I discovered the remains of our cows, their entrails dried out on banana leaves. I tried to take in the violence that had taken place here.

In one of the destroyed houses I noticed some books. I bent over and … saw the books and notebooks of my children. A huge shock jolted through me. Their names were on the cover. When I read them, I became very upset and emotional. I began to tremble, my whole body shaking, as I screamed my children's names. Sobbing, I repeated their names over and over again.

The soldier who was with me was concerned about me and my obvious distress. After I had managed to get my emotions somewhat under control, he persuaded me to leave, to allow the shock and my feelings of confusion to sink in first before returning another day.

Still in shock, expressionless, I walked with the soldier up the hill where we met an old Hutu neighbour, Naason, who greeted me and immediately began describing in detail the deaths of my children, my mother-in-law, my sister-in-law and her child, and many of our Tutsi neighbours. However, I had the undeniable feeling that he wasn't telling the complete truth. He didn't name any of the perpetrators, nor name those who had destroyed our houses and slaughtered our livestock. He played dumb: "I really don't know who did that. I just heard about it from others. I didn't see anything myself."

Oh no? Could he really not have seen what happened in broad daylight? Was he threatened? No, of course not.

He was willing to walk with us to show me the place where people had died. He went on ahead and let us see the place where the slaughter had taken place, but he didn't point out the place where the perpetrators had left the bodies. Silent and full of sorrow, we went back and on the way we met only stray dogs.

As we walked through Gihisi, we were witness to a dramatic scene. Dogs were dragging the body of a dead child across the road and looked like they were going to tear it into pieces. In a fit of anger, I grabbed a couple of stones and threw them at the wild dogs. They jumped back, whimpering, and left the little body lying on the ground. Around the back of an abandoned house, we discovered a small pickaxe against the wall. I took it with me.

The soldier, who was wearing a cloth around his neck, took it off and wrapped the child up in it. With the pickaxe we dug a pit and carefully lay the child in it to give it a dignified burial.

Death imposed itself upon us in all its gruesome ways. Not only in the form of dead bodies, but also in the pungent smell of decomposition caused by the corpses lying strewn about.

We walked on to Nsengiyumva's house. During my absence the family had taken good care of Lambert. I was very happy about that because he had missed out on a lot of much-needed care in the previous few months. I had become used to being cautious, to being on the run with the constant fear of being discovered and murdered. It was only now that it began to dawn on me that there was no longer any need for us to fear for our lives. I found something to sit on. I had to allow the fact that we were safe to sink in; I had to accept the dangers we had survived; I had to cope with all the horrors to which we had either been witness or almost victim. I had to accept that I'd lost everything and had nothing left.

No sooner had I sat down when I was overwhelmed by an intense wave of trauma. I was possessed by heavy emotions. When Lambert came to greet me, I pushed him away from me and I spoke in an accusatory tone that all my children were dead, even my eldest. There is a saying in Rwanda: 'Ubuze imfura ata ibiheko': 'They who lose their eldest child, lose their expectations.'

I felt wronged and disappointed; all hope was gone. This is what I now burdened Lambert with. A baby of a little more than one year old, who of course understood absolutely nothing of what I was saying to him.

Early in the morning, I walked unaccompanied back to the remnants of my house. Even though I could now walk on the road without the fear that something could happen to me, I still felt desperate. I felt very gloomy and wondered if it really wouldn't be better to die. This trauma caused such huge despair and insecurity in my life. "What meaning can my life have without my husband? What can I expect from a life without my children? Who am I without my friends?" That was my reasoning as I went on my way in my heavy mood. The negative mood and pessimistic thoughts caused such depressing feelings that they took control of my mental faculties and I lost sight of all reason. I felt myself going insane; I lost my senses. I ran in all directions, crazy, with my hands in the air, screaming out all of my sorrow and misery.

In spite of these panic attacks I eventually managed to arrive at my destroyed house and I really hoped to run into Naason again. Unfortunately, I didn't see him so I walked over to his house. There I found only his wife. She informed me that her husband had thought it better for his own safety to flee to Congo.

I suspected that his reason for leaving was to also warn his family and friends of the possible consequences of returning home, since I was still alive and the camp was under the protection of the RPF soldiers. They were under the misapprehension that I had died in the Gatagara massacre.

While I still stood talking to Naason's wife, we were surprised by the terrible sound of rounds being fired and the short sharp rick-tick echoing of automatic weapons further along, immediately followed by loud calling and shouting. It turned out to be a branch of the Interahamwe trying to regain their lost positions. RPF soldiers came running up, gesturing and calling to residents to head back to the camp at Mugandamure since it was safer there. One of the soldiers left his unit in order to escort us to the camp.

When I was safely back in the camp, I noticed that many people were busy packing up their baggage. They intended to make their way to Mayaga, where they hoped to find a less dangerous refugee camp.

Further ahead I saw Lambert running and there I also saw the Nsengiyumva family, who were also preparing to leave. They offered to take Lambert with them and to take care of him, since I was so traumatised. But I refused.

I decided to head out on the road to Mayaga as well, a road upon which the stream of uprooted people advanced slowly and with difficulty, almost tripping over each other, weighed down with baggage: mattresses, provisions, tools, furniture and other belongings.

And me? I only had a child in my arms. People asked me: "Why did you leave all your things at home?" I could only give them one answer: I had lost everything because my neighbours had stolen all of my possessions.

We spent the first night in Kirundo, the second in Gati and the night after that we slept in Nyundo. These were all new names to me because I had never set foot in Mayaga. We eventually arrived at Rwabusoro, a military camp, where we stayed for a short time. We slept in the open air, which for me was no problem since Lambert and I had become used to nothing else during the previous months. I had greater concerns. What to think about my future? Would I have a chance to live my life in an acceptable and responsible way?

The following morning some people from our group walked onwards to Bugesera and from there to Kigali. I really didn't feel like going any further and I asked a soldier if I could stay on with them. He could sense my hopelessness and even went looking for accommodation for me. His search led him to some people who had also survived the massacres. In a nearby refugee camp he found the family of Edison and his wivve Ruth, who were prepared to take me in. The soldier took us to them.

But in the camp where I now found myself, I discovered to my horror it wasn't actually so safe after all. The Interahamwe regularly carried out dangerous surprise attacks in order to regain lost territory. In the hills surrounding the camp, people searching for food or wood were killed by stray bullets in these exchanges of fire. Landmines too, placed in abandoned houses by Hutus, exploded when unsuspecting refugees, thinking they'd found themselves a hiding place, accidentally detonated them. In the refugee camp a great number of people also tragically died from dysentery after drinking contaminated water.

Personally, I became ever more convinced that God was keeping His eye on me. I had begged Him to keep me alive so that, after the liberation, I could personally bear witness to the end of the bloody atrocities.

In spite of my having survived the slaughter, every day was torture for me, partly because of the memories of my family. Images of my husband and children constantly appeared before me. In my thoughts I imagined the horrifying last moments of my children and I heard them screaming: "Mama! Mama!"

After the genocide my thoughts were confirmed when I heard that one of them called out, immediately before he was murdered: "I'll tell my mum! Don't kill me before I've seen my mum! I'm going to tell her that you want to kill me, but that I've done nothing wrong!" One of the killers then took his machete and contemptuously grinned at the others: "Do you hear what the little snake says!" And with a mocking laugh he hacked my child's head off in one go. It was my son, Olivier. I heard this years later when one of the killers confessed this crime before the gacaca.

At the beginning of July, the population was called upon to return to their own houses. It was a moment that many had been waiting for and everyone had been looking forward to.

The order applied not only to those families that had survived the massacres, but also to all Hutus on the run who had not fled to Congo.

But where could I go, I wondered. I had no home anymore. Worse still, I had nothing at all. In desperation, I sought help with the soldiers and asked them if I could stay there with them. The soldier who had brought me to Edison and Ruth would only be able to make a decision about that when there was a guarantee of safety in the area. The Interahamwe were still hiding out in the forests nearby.

Eventually, together with Edison and his family, I left for Gatagara, their home town. There were four dead bodies lying by their front door. Edison hesitated, unsure what to do, but soon took a pickaxe and buried the bodies. After that grim find I refused to sleep inside that house and suggested looking for shelter elsewhere. We succeeded. We managed to find another place to sleep for the night.

The following morning we walked on to Ruhango, 25 kilometres south of Gitarama.

During our stay there the RPF soldiers shared their biscuits and soap. They also gave us ever more hope that we were going to be safe from the killers. The intensity of the fighting abated and our chances for survival grew.

Coincidentally, among the people I was on the road from camp to camp with was one of my parent's neighbours. He was also a refugee. From him I received dramatic news about my mother, who had found herself in the company of a group with whom this neighbour had also gone on the run. Many of the group had fallen victim to the ruthless methods of the murderers who had captured them. People were hacked to pieces and had their body parts thrown into the Nyabarongo river. Others, among them my mother, were thrown in latrines. And even more had been liquidated on the road when they attempted to flee to Burundi.

When I heard all the horrific details, I felt the blood drain from my face. I turned to stone and shouted out: "I don't give a damn anymore! It's all over! Let me die!" Then I lost consciousness and collapsed to the ground, like a tree that is felled and torn away from its roots.

A stream of stories ensued. Constantly we received new information. We were continually overwhelmed with sad news about family and friends. Our ears were really only tuned to receive terrible news.

A month later I went to visit my husband's brother, Innocent. I walked up the hill with him to his house. Innocent was an open man and on our way up, he greeted everyone he met or he had a short chat with them. My sorrow was so great, however, that I just couldn't find it within me to greet people. I cried: "I'm so distraught. They have killed so many of my relatives! How did you know I'd not been murdered?"

Innocent answered me. Someone had told him that they had seen me among a group of survivors and he found out that I was staying with the Edison family. Now he wanted to take me with him to Kigali to find Sylvie, his sister. She was also still alive. However, I didn't accept his proposal.

I wanted to go to Nyanza first since I wasn't far from there. I could always go to Kigali later.

In Nyanza I hoped to find the bodies of my beloved family members and to ensure they were given a dignified resting place.

My brother-in-law Innocent went to Kigali, but promised to return to Nyanza. I went on alone to visit again the places where we had lived. A few neighbours who had also returned and who saw me coming set off in the other direction. They were afraid of my vengeance, because I had seen them by the checkpoint, or I'd seen them pass by while I was hiding in the bushes.

By asking around, I eventually found the place where the dead from our village had been thrown and abandoned. All of these victims had been killed at the 'Progrès' shopping centre. 'Future', a promising name when the centre had been built; now an ironic name, because 'Progrès' had evolved into a place of misery, death and gruesome killings.

After I had convinced myself that the dead really were lying at that particular spot near 'Progrès', I made a little mound with a load of sand, as is done with real graves, and I planted flowers there, which would help me to find this piece of land again later. By making mounds I also wanted to prevent dogs from digging up the bodies to eat them, or at least make it more difficult for them since they had made this their daily habit.

After that I went back to the refugee camp in Ruhango where I met Innocent again, who promised to accompany me to Kigali, to his sister. Innocent and Sylvie were the only survivors from my husband's family. I said goodbye to the Edison family and thanked them for their wonderful support and good care.

Still without baggage, we took the bus to Kigali and our destination was the small district of Kabeza, where I met up again with my sister-in-law and her eight month-old baby. Her welcome was heartwarming, but the circumstances in which we now met caused us only sorrow and tears. Crying, we spoke about the future and wondered what kind of a future awaited us after everything that we had endured. Was it still possible for us to lead a normal life? Wouldn't it be better for us both - and this is something we were very honest with each other about - wouldn't we both be better off dead than living this pathetic life?

These were the somber thoughts running through our heads, pushed to the side every now and then only by our everyday concerns.

Murambi genocide memorial.
'We cannot forget our loved ones.'

His Excellency Paul Kagame, the current president of Rwanda. He was the commander of the RPF liberation army that ended the genocide against the Tutsi.

THE FIRST CONTACT WITH SOLACE MINISTRIES

Along with our children, Sylvie and I lived for two months rent-free in the house where Innocent had put us up. Then the owner came to tell us that from then on we'd have to pay 30,000 Rwandan francs a month. Innocent didn't have a problem with that because he had started work again a while before. Three months later, however, the owner sold the house and we moved to Remera, a quarter of Kigali, where we moved into a house that Innocent had bought. I still live there now.

What I can remember from that period are the terrible nights ('nuits blanches'). I went through hell and was unable to sleep. As soon as I turned off the light and closed my eyes, the appalling memories came flooding back. If the mercilessly brutal murderers were in pursuit, I started shouting: "Oh! Oh, they're coming to kill us!" I heard the helpless voices of panicking victims and the screaming of the children; I was haunted by images of stray dogs looking for corpses to devour. It all raced through my mind. It was so intense that I yelled out in fear. All night long I was scared to death. That fear had such a hold over me that, from that time onwards, I needed to leave the light on in the room to avoid the darkness, the darkness where numerous grim memories loomed and only intensified my fear.

Mindful living was made impossible for me and a lot just passed me by. My thoughts were dominated by the murderers' ruthless brutal misdeeds and the violent deaths of the victims.

In spite of this painfully dark period, I managed to make the acquaintance of some other female teachers who had also survived the genocide. They set about convincing me to take up my former profession and to look for a job with APAPER, a primary school where they also taught class.

But now there were new problems. I couldn't find my diploma because all of my possessions had been stolen, destroyed or burned. And even so, how could I, in God's name, stand before a class full of children who reminded me of my own murdered children? Or who evoked memories of my former pupils who had been killed, but also of those pupils who had killed? I didn't see how I could do it, but my colleagues were persistent. They assured me that I could always call on them if I needed to.

One morning I went to APAPER and during a conversation with the directors, I expressed my doubts. They were very understanding and very cooperative, and shortly afterwards I was able to start teaching.

I started with a class of 38 pupils with whom I quickly built up a good and friendly rapport. Most children were survivors of the genocide and many of them had lost both parents. Many more had scars from the massacres, such as those caused by a machete, or from grenade shrapnel that had penetrated their bodies following an explosion.

The first days were tough and there were many tears, but despite this I did my absolute best to comfort these shaken and damaged young people and I constantly encouraged them to dedicate themselves to completing their studies as best they could. After all, a solid education would provide them with the chance to get their young lives back on course, lives during which they had already encountered so much misery.

We got through the year very well with each other, and were able to offer each other comfort and consolation. And in the exams they attained outstanding results. Good results not only within the school, but also when compared to the results of the other sectors.

At the end of 1994, about six months after the genocide, I met Placide's niece Drocella Nduwimana in Kigali. Drocella had only been married a year when her husband was murdered. When we fell into each other's arms, all the sorrow of the death and the absence of our husbands resurfaced. We both had a lot of tears to shed and as she cried she told me that she had fled to Burundi, together with her three sisters, Scholas, Beatrice and Dusabe, and her two brothers-in-law, Kayiranga and Karangwa. In Burundi they awaited the end of the genocide. In those two hours that we spent together, we felt like victims sharing a close, warm bond, especially when we spoke about the terrible massacres that our neighbours had on their consciences. What had happened to us seemed so unreal to us, it was as if we had lived in another time, in another world, in hell even. It was unfathomable and indescribable!

Our conversation suddenly took another turn when Drocella mentioned the name Jean Gakwandi, a man who also turned out to be a genocide survivor. This Jean saw his survival as a sign from God and considered it now to be his calling to help widows and orphans. He had found a temporary place in Kigali where under his leadership regular gatherings took place with these victims. Jean gave these meetings the name Solace Ministries.

"What happens at these meetings then? What is the point of them all coming together?" I asked, full of curiosity. Drocella explained to me that Jean encouraged them all, in spite of any feelings of sadness or grief, to carry on with their lives again and certainly not to give up. He gave the women words of courage and encouraged them to be strong, to show strength. With him you had the chance and the time to talk about your deepest misery, about all the great suffering that you had had to bear. The power of the meetings lay mostly in pouring out your heart, bringing feelings to the surface, freeing yourself of the painful stifling sorrow. By verbalising the pitiful state of your life, you could express your sorrow and grief for the painful loss you had had to endure during the previous months.

Jean was inspired by the word of God. To the women he demonstrated His Spirit, which gave hope to all, who had protected them and had performed mysterious things before their eyes, in spite of all misery and danger.

Drocella invited me: "Come to a meeting with me some time. I'm sure you'd find it helpful. And then you'll be able to see where the meetings are held." It seemed to be worth the effort and I agreed. On the appointed day, Drocella came to pick me up very early in the morning and we took a minibus from Remera to the center. Then on foot we climbed for five hundred metres before we eventually came to some houses. Between two of these houses there was a wide pathway where a group of women were sitting. There were also long benches, covered with banana leaves, one after another. So the meetings took place in the open air. "And if it rains?" Drocella explained that if it happened to rain, they put up a canvas so that no one got wet. And if anyone complained about the rain then that woman was told: "Just think of April 1994!" And that put an end to the complaints.

I saw an animated and enthusiastic man praying in front of a group of eight women. Drocella and I seated ourselves on the bench behind them. After praying we got to know each other and we embraced everyone. I watched the women attentively, their faces etched with sorrow. I asked Drocella gently who the women were. She whispered: "They are the widows I told you about." "And that man?" I wanted to know. "That is Jean Gakwandi! Quiet. Listen!" Jean welcomed me very warmly and introduced everyone to me. He told me his name was Jean Gakwandi and that he was a survivor of the genocide. Sadly though, his parents had died, as had his brothers and other family members. In the months following the genocide he had strongly felt the need to pray and he regularly begged for God's mercy. God had given him a task, he revealed to us, which you could find in the Bible in Isaiah, chapter 40, verse 1: "Comfort, comfort my people." And inspired by these words, he began his vocation, the mission of God: bringing hope and peace into the lives, so inhumanely violated, of widows and orphans.

After Jean had spoken, the women introduced themselves to me. They told me their names, told me where they lived and also spoke briefly about what they'd been through during the genocide. I felt it was enough for this first meeting to tell them my name and where I lived.

Then Jean spoke again and read us a passage from Isaiah, chapter 41, verse 10: "Fear not, for I am with you; be not dismayed, for I am your God." These words really gripped me and I looked at Jean with great eyes. Jean read another passage, in which God reassures widows and orphans, and which can be found in Exodus, chapter 22, verses 22-23: "Do not take advantage of the widow or the fatherless. If you do and they cry out to me, I will certainly hear their cry." Jean clarified these words: "If you have lost everyone and you have nothing, then God says: I will be there to help you get through it."

The meeting came to an end and Jean, while saying goodbye, asked if anyone needed us to pray together for anything. I admitted that I'd not been able to sleep since the genocide. The stifling fear of the murderers held me tightly in its grip. I constantly saw the images of my children before me, while the terrible screaming and the desperate voices of the murdered victims penetrated deep into my being. Jean laid his hands on my head and he prayed so passionately for me that the women began to cry. Jean prayed to God that there would be peace throughout our land; he prayed for all of the widows and orphans; he asked God to help these people by easing and taking away their sorrow and suffering. After the prayer, Jean made another appointment with us for the following meeting.

We walked back home and a curious Drocella asked me what my first impressions were. I reacted enthusiastically. I had really been able to find some comfort in seeing other widows and sharing my experiences with them. The moment I met Jean had made a deep impression on me. It even seemed as though I had been freed from the obsession of thinking only about death and the dead. It was as if I were free of the fear that consumed me. The word of God brought salvation and I felt faith rising within me, that God would make true the promise of his words. But truth be told, I was also left with a number of pressing questions: would it be possible for our wounds, carved so deeply into our souls, to ever heal? How? Drocella accompanied me home and the two of us also arranged to meet again for the following meeting.

That evening I went to bed. And how miraculous! The night after that first meeting with Jean, I slept right through until the morning. His prayer had been answered!

My sister-in-law Sylvie, who lived with me, was surprised and asked how it was possible that I had managed to get such a good night's sleep. With subdued joy, I confided in her that Drocella had taken me to a place where widows met with each other, under the leadership of a man, a survivor, called Jean. That this Jean supported the women and encouraged them to climb out of the dark valley of sorrow and to conquer their inner pain. And that this Jean prayed for the widows and also for me: "I've had a good night's sleep for the first time in a long time. Isn't that a miracle? His prayer has been answered!"

I attended the second meeting alone, without Drocella, because she was busy that day. During this gathering the widows in turn shared what they had been through. The others were so compassionate and felt their suffering to such a degree that they also had to cry.

Women walked around or sat on the ground; some were on their knees. Some were grieving because they no longer had children. They had all been killed. Other women showed the scars of the machetes and nailed clubs they had been beaten halfway to death with. Other widows turned out to be so traumatised that they could only mumble unintelligible words. And there were also those who said nothing, as silent as a grave.

Most were thinking of their own sorrows. Resurfacing memories of horrific moments translated into heartbreaking despair. The cries of sorrow went hand in hand with extreme, repetitive gestures. Some beat themselves on the head, others on their thighs. The women stamped on the ground, trembled and screamed it out.

"What complete and absolute bastards those neighbours were!" someone shouted.

"How were our children, our husbands, our parents killed?" cried another.

A woman prayed: "Help us! Help us, God Almighty!"

All the misery and sorrow came flooding out. The hellish pain of these violent memories came from so deep within their hearts, it was screamed out in an assortment of the same words repeated over and over again: "How long must we bear this pain?"

"Oh, when will our suffering come to an end?"

"Would it not be better for me to be dead than still alive!?"

"My husband is dead and I will never see him again!"

Distraught, the women put their hands on their heads and walked around in a daze.

Jean showed a lot of respect for the women's sorrow, allowed them to express their own intensely painful feelings and walked among the group passionately praying. He also attempted to lighten the mood by singing hymns expressing hope.

I still have very warm memories of Hymn 149 from the hymn book, a song that really expresses God's love. Both the melody and the words carried me away so much that I felt hope and peace; yes, a peaceful calm in my heart. Something was growing there, slowly things were turning around and I felt that a seed had been sowed there. Seeds had been scattered for a process that would put me in a condition to heal myself of my trauma.

One day the Solace Ministries group moved to a new location. Having previously held our meetings in the open air, in an alley between two houses, we would now be gathering in the Kacyiru district in the building of World Relief, a religious social work organisation. This organisation rented offices where various activities took place. Not so surprising then that we were able to move there since Jean worked for this international institution. Together or individually, the regular sessions with the widows and orphans continued and it was noticeable that the number of participants quickly grew. We went from eight to twelve people, to fifteen, forty people!! Whenever I bumped into widows I knew on the street, we spoke about when we would see each other again at Jean Gakwandi's. Those meetings we christened 'Chez Gakwandi.' We were able to be ourselves there and we could cry and pour our hearts out over the loss of our dear husbands, children and other family members.

The more often we gathered together, the more our strength returned. We felt ourselves becoming stronger. Very slowly and little by little, we started to become human again, physically as well as mentally.

One time Jean invited his friend Emmanuël Ngoga and his wife Mary to talk to us about the word of God and to comfort us. We grew close as a group and felt so at one with each other that we came to consider ourselves as one family in which we saw each other as sisters and brothers.

One day in 1995 I went to Jean for individual counselling. He asked me what he could do to help me because World Relief was an organisation that offered practical support to people so that they could piece their lives back together.

They wanted to help victims to regain their self-esteem and feel that they had a contribution to make to society. Corrugated sheets, tools, clothing, food and other materials were distributed, with which people could go about rebuilding their lives. Many survivors and refugees who returned from abroad and had no possessions at all, not even a home, received help in this way and they were given the chance to get their lives back on track.

I didn't visit Jean to ask for anything material, however. My request was of a different nature. I asked him if he would pray for me. His prayer to let me sleep peacefully again had been answered. I was sleeping a lot better, but the whole day through I was constantly reminded of the terrible events, the appalling memories that dominated my thoughts. Severely intrusive images against which I had no defence. I didn't know a normal life any longer; the ability to think like a normal human was strange to me. All the killing, the death of my husband, my children and my parents: they were holding me back in my daily life. Would Jean please pray for me to banish those awful compulsive thoughts?

I took photographs of my daughters, Joyeuse and Claudette, out from my bag, and when I showed them to Jean, I became emotional and I burst into tears. Jean looked at the photographs, was deeply shocked, began to cry and called out: "Yoh! My God! Are even these innocent children dead!" He comforted me and asked me expressly to have the courage to live my life. I promised I would do my best.

It was such an unforgettable experience, meeting someone who showed himself to be so deeply compassionate and empathetic, who showed me his sorrow by openly shedding his tears over the deaths of my children. This gave me a lot of faith. I felt grateful and happy that someone was willing to take the time to pray for me!

We made a new appointment for a chat and at the following meeting, I learned from Jean, together with his wife Viviane, the amazing story of a strong woman named Ruth.

Naomi, a Jewish woman, had fled from Israel with her husband and two sons because of the severe famine. In the foreign land, her husband died and a short time afterwards her two sons, who had married local women, also die. One of the women is called Ruth. Naomi decides to return to Israel, accompanied by her two daughters-in-law. One of the women, however, decides to head back to her own country. Only Ruth remains loyal to Naomi and they go on together to Israel. The two women have a difficult time, but they don't give up. On the contrary! They struggle through the difficult time. Without family, in spite of poverty, their sorrow over their dead husbands, they persevere and give their lives meaning. Their courage is rewarded. Ruth finds happiness with her new husband, Boaz, and so provides Naomi with a new family: a new son(-in-law) and a year later a grandson. This story illustrates how keeping hope alive, even if difficult at times, brings its rewards.

Mary Ngoga acquainted us with another such strong character from the Bible: Job. Job was a man with amazing willpower and great faith in God, in spite of all the obstacles put in his way. Job, who lost all of his children within a short time, who lost all of his possessions and also became seriously ill, remained steadfast in his belief in God! And God? He did not betray Job's faith and repaid Job many times over.

It became clear to me that the Bible describes people who struggle against adversity and misfortune, and especially how they deal with those obstacles. I realized that the Bible contained far more than I had believed and decided to study the book. During my reading of the Bible I came to understand what Isaac had meant with his words, when he had given me that Bible during the genocide. I felt an ever growing need to take the Bible and to seek out examples that could offer me comfort in my misery. And there are many examples in which you can find God when you are in sorrow.

When I came home, I would enthusiastically relate the inspiring life lessons I had learned at Solace Ministries. But I also became aware that I had to dare to confront my past in order to be able to deal with it and accept it. I had to accept this fatal and terrible past in order to give it an appropriate place in my life. Only then would I be able to accept the present, in order to start thinking constructively about my future.

After the genocide again in front of the class at the APAPER school in Kigali.

I started as a volunteer with Solace Ministries in 2000.

MY LOST CHILDREN

After the RPF liberated us, the genocide still held many of us captive in its astoundingly oppressive grasp. It was a confounding and turbulent time. Every day, the country was plunged deeper and deeper into mourning, as the horror of the extent of the massacres became clearer and more shocking: so dramatic, so unfathomable.

Despite my deep sadness I searched for ways to recover some thread of life again; to give meaning to the days and months of that terrible year 1994; to somehow push my trauma aside.

I found a strand of thread thanks to the help that Solace Ministries offered me, and I also found a strand of thread in my work at the school.

But I still had a hold of one strand of thread: taking care of my child, which I had a hold on even during the genocide. Though shortly after the genocide, that responsibility of caring for one child unexpectedly grew into caring for several more children. Not just for Lambert but also for my son Dieudonné and later for my little daughter Denise, children that I thought had been killed during the genocide.

Soon after the genocide, I took four more children in, namely two of my brother's children: Donatien and Eugenie and two of my sister's children: Françoise and Francine, because their parents had sadly been murdered. My circumstances didn't make raising kids any easier. I tried to make the best of what was an arduous and difficult task, partly with thanks to the support of others.

Each day, the loss of my husband, children, family and many

people dear to me affected my life in an immensely depressing way. Shortly after the RPF ended the atrocities in the country, I knew one thing for sure: my youngest child Lambert and I were alive. I no longer believed that I would see the others alive again; I had given up that hope.

However, my conviction that all of my children had been killed was called into question, shortly after the end of the genocide, when I was still living in a refugee camp. Some hopeful news about Dieudonné, my nine-year-old son, began to trickle in.
The boy had fled with his grandmother and some other older people. Along the way, the whole group had been surrounded by members of the Interahamwe and driven into a yard, where a small Hutu army was waiting for them and began hacking away at them. The Tutsis didn't stand a chance and fell victim to the ruthless machetes. Only my son, Dieudonné, managed to escape the massacre by diving through a small opening in the fence just in time. Distraught, he knocked on the door of a vicarage, where an Italian priest gave him shelter and a hiding place under a bed. When Hutus came to the priest's door to ask where the little Tutsi went, he adamantly denied having even one Tutsi in the house. After the genocide it turned out that he had allowed no less than 40 Tutsi children to hide there. The priest had family in Italy and wanted to send Dieudonné there for his own safety, because he was convinced that the Hutus had murdered the little boy's family. How did I find all this out? I met one of my neighbour's sons, Xavier, a soldier who served in the RPF-liberation army and he told me that he had seen a child who looked a lot like Dieudonné. I didn't want to believe him and I refuted his claim, steadfast. "All my children are dead!" I declared, through my tears. But Xavier remained adamant that he had seen Dieudonné with a priest.
My hope was rekindled and I praised the Lord, for if it was true that my son was still alive, I was ready to surrender to Him completely and bear witness to His greatness.
I went to visit the priest as quickly as possible, but he wasn't going to return the child, my child, just like that.

"I've heard from reliable sources that everyone in his family is dead," he said and he pointed out that several others had visited him to claim the child as theirs. I had to demonstrate that this boy was really my child. He wanted proof. I had to answer extensive questions about where I lived; he wanted exact details about my husband, about brothers and sisters and other family members. Why wasn't I dead?

"This is my child. I want to take him with me!" I cried. During the examination my trauma reemerged, especially as I recounted the inhumane acts that I'd witnessed. Did the reverend priest even know what had happened in Rwanda over the last few months? The horrific experiences that I described to him certainly made it clear! I brought up all of the atrocities to which I had borne witness. It was not only my answers to his questions, but also my gruesome stories, that seemed to convince him that I really had to be the boy's mother.

However, since there was still so much chaos and uncertainty in our country at that time, the priest still refused to give Dieudonné to me. Was it even safe or responsible of me to take my young son? Two weeks later, I was finally allowed to take Dieudonné into my gleeful embrace and he went with me to the refugee camp.

Then there's my daughter Denise, aged seven. I had also lived with the assumption that she was dead, until someone addressed me about her.

"Do you know that one of your daughters was brought to safety by a certain Ziripa? They both went to Congo and they live there in the woods now."

Oh, my heart broke. I was overjoyed, but very anxious at the same time. "She won't survive that. She'll catch a disease like cholera and die like so many people who fled there."

I prayed and prayed to God who had saved me, who had spared Lambert and Dieudonné: "Let Denise survive too!"

Unfortunately, I didn't hear anything else about her until the beginning of 1996 when many Hutus and Tutsis began to return from Congo.

"Your daughter was seen with Ziripa and RPF soldiers."
The RPF soldiers were assigned to bring as many Tutsi refugees back to Rwanda from Congo as possible. When they were monitoring the repatriates, the soldiers became skeptical as to whether Ziripa was really Denise's mother because of the difference in their skin color. Denise was adamant that Ziripa was her mother, but she added that she had had another mother in Rwanda who was no longer alive.
"So what was your mother's name?" the soldier asked.
"My mother was called Beata, but she, Ziripa, is my mother now!"
The soldiers took Denise, Ziripa and many others back to Rwanda in trucks. Denise went to live with the family of a certain Oriose. One day, a merchant came to tell me that Denise had returned from Congo alive, and where I could find her. I quickly went to the address and met her in the yard. She didn't recognize me. But I wasn't afraid that she'd never remember me. Denise just needed time to process all those confusing and shocking events of her so very young life. When she had fled she had been five years old, and now she was seven. I took my little daughter home with me, nurtured her lovingly and we talked about our memories together. Slowly our bond grew and Denise grew to believe that I was really her mother. Not dead, but alive.

The year 1996 invokes still more intense and emotional memories for me. Beside the joy of having found my children, I was living with the painful idea that my husband and five other children were dead. Their absence was very painful for me. Above all, the fact that I didn't know where their bodies were cut right through my soul. The slightest news rekindled my hope that I might find the bodies of my dead husband, children and other beloved family members. I kept searching and searching but to no avail. The uncertainty of the situation weighed heavily on my soul.
Things only became clearer when many of the killers returned from Congo. Some of them directed us to the places where we could find discarded bodies.

On any day or week that I was free, I travelled towards Nyanza with this new information in the back of my mind. Strengthened by renewed hope, I began to look for my children in different places and I managed to find their remains spread out over several locations and amongst other people's remains. The dead were not always in the ground either, and the bodies that we found in latrines were beginning to decompose too. When I was searching and digging in the earth, I was constantly confronted with a feeling of utter devastation. So confronting!

One day I came across a body and dug it out very carefully. To my great dismay, the body turned out to be my daughter, Joyeuse. Her murderers had cut off her head and stuffed it into her vest. I found Claudette too, with her hands missing. They had been cut off. Having seen so many mutilated bodies, I had to conclude that the killers kept coming up with sadistic ways for each victim to meet a gruesome death.

Besides Joyeuse and Claudette, I later dug up the bodies of my three other murdered children: Germain, Olivier and Rutayisire. I cried with such sorrow for the happiness we had lost.

Germain, whose last wave, his farewell at the roadblock, is still so vivid in my memory; whose sincere voice I can still hear.

My children, young people with such enthusiastic plans before the genocide, full of ideals, unaware of the gruesome violence that would bring their lives and their futures to such an abrupt end.

My children with expectations and dreams for the future:
my daughter Joyeuse's dream to be a social worker;
my daughter Claudette's dream to be a doctor;
my son Germain's dream to be an engineer;
my son Olivier's dream to be a lawyer;
my son Rutayisire's dream to be a priest.

All their dreams, ruthlessly disrupted in their youth; abruptly and gruesomely demolished.

All I had was their dead bodies now.

I now bore the weight of a heavy and emotional task: burying my murdered children.

Every time I dug up and placed bodies back together - which Innocent came from Kigali to help me do - we took the remains to the reburial area. In doing so, we had to make sure that the dogs didn't defile the bodies by digging them up and mauling them.

I ordered coffins for my children. We found the bodies of my mother-in-law, my sister-in-law and one of my husband's nephews and I also got coffins for them in Ruhango.

Innocent and I also bought coffins in Ruhango for other victims we found when searching for our families. It seemed only right to re-bury these dead people too, this time with the respect that they deserved. Innocent and I also covered the bulk of the cost of their coffins and re-burials, since many of the victims had no surviving family. Besides, there were victims who had been fleeing from other regions, who had ended up in our area, so they didn't have any family or acquaintances here. Even when we did manage to track down victims' relatives, they usually couldn't afford to pay all the re-burial costs anyway.

In the end we had dug up 347 bodies and seventeen heads whose bodies we were unable to find.

When I had fulfilled what was my sad duty, I returned home. I lived in the house in Kigali, which Innocent had bought for us after the genocide, and I stayed there for nearly two years, caring for seven children.

The searches affected me deeply and put me under great strain. Exhuming bodies and reburying them was time consuming and left me feeling so vulnerable that it inhibited me from teaching properly. Due to my unstable state of mind, I decided to resign from APAPER.

I was unemployed for two months when Gervais, a friend of my husband, came to visit me. He told me about a job opening at CESTRAR, the National Workers Insurance Institute. They were looking for an employee for their 'Union des Caisses' department in Remera, where I lived. Gervais advised me to write a job application letter, which he would deliver personally, since he worked at CESTRAR too.

A week later I received an offer from them, and I started work right away. I did so well at work that the personnel manager at the 'Union des Caisses' offered me a contract, which was signed with mutual consent. I was also able to do some training there and having taken an exam in 1998, I was appointed the manager and processer of financial affairs and accounts. I liked the work and I was fully committed to it. The clients who came to my counter were very positive about my work as well as my pleasant and helpful service.

Although I was very happy with my new job, in which I was able to help other people, my fondest memories were still of my former occupation as a teacher. I hadn't taught for twenty-six years for nothing.

I worked at CESTRAR from 1997-2000, where everything went well. In the year 2000, at the beginning of my annual leave, I was on my way to the 'Rwandan Social Funds' office to pick up my husband's pension when I bumped into Jean Gakwandi, who had been of immense help to me after the genocide. His sessions had given me faith again. Since I went to the meetings regularly as part of my therapy, I quickly began to develop a clear picture of his counselling approach. Jean had noticed this too and he soon suggested that I assist him in the widows' meetings. I did so in 1995, a few times.

So Jean and I knew each other well. We walked together and were soon talking about the activities at Solace Ministries and Jean invited me to come and work with him again during my vacation. I accepted his offer and spent my weeks off working at Solace Ministries as a counsellor.

Widows and orphans came to the consultations; I listened to them, gave them advice and counselled them through their recovery therapy, thereby assisting in their healing process. Being able to mean so much to these people through social work gave me a lot of satisfaction as well as an intense feeling of happiness. I found it such a blessing to see that survivors could begin to bloom again, because I was willing to listen to them and give them the opportunity to share their testimony with me.

On behalf of Solace Ministries, I also went to see widows in their homes, to see for myself how hard life was alone, without family. An important part of my job ended up being to create a new family for widows and orphans, who were now alone.

When my vacation time was over, Jean suggested that I continue to work at Solace Ministries. I agreed to continue, mostly because these women, particularly the widows, were a reflection of my own life and my own past. Counselling also really appealed to me and I felt confident that I had the right qualities for the job.

Jean took care of some organizational affairs for me, such as creating a program, organizing the consultations and house visits.

I started making work visits to women in Kigali. Later I began to visit women in Kimironko, Busanza, Nyagasambu, Nyamata, Nyanza, Bicumbi and many other places, and my work became more and more extensive. But I still had my paid job with CESTRAR and as a result, I wasn't always available for sessions at Solace Ministries.

Finally, I had to make a choice, and in 2002 I decided to leave CESTRAR. I tendered my resignation and I signed a permanent contract with Solace Ministries. From then on I was responsible for the 'Counselling Department.' I had my own office, where I could receive widows and orphans for individual counselling, but my work also comprised group therapy sessions.

I had a memorable meeting back when I was working as a volunteer for Jean. Isaac visited me. He had heard from his neighbours that I lived in Remera and that I was active at Solace Ministries in my free time. Isaac was the Adventist who had given Lambert and me a place of refuge to protect us from the murderous genocidaires. He had survived the genocide, along with his daughter. He told me that when we were forced to leave his house, he had had an extremely strong feeling that Lambert and I would survive the violence. When he had heard that I was indeed still alive and that this strong feeling had not betrayed him, he felt the need to come and find me at Solace Ministries. We spoke with each other about our experiences during the genocide and I told him how we had miraculously survived the violence, not least thanks to his Bible. I also told him about the miserable fate that I had had to face and how I ended up at Solace Ministries. He expressed his regret that my life had taken such a dramatic turn and promised to pray that the future would bring me hope and faith.

Our daughter Claudette who dreamed of becoming a doctor.

Our son Germain who dreamed of becoming an engineer.

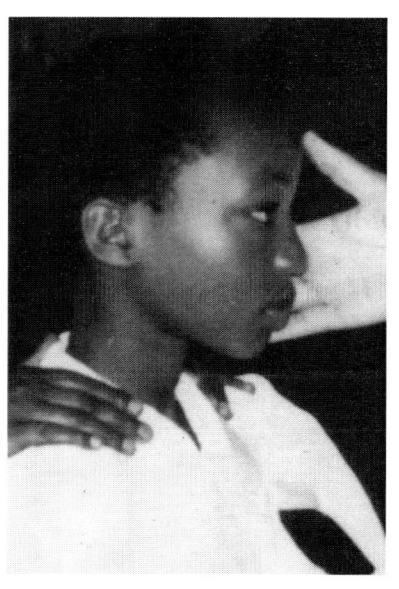

Our daughter Joyeuse who dreamed of becoming a social worker.

*Nyagatovu, the place where I was born and where I lived with my parents.
After the genocide this was left of it.*

FORGIVE IN ORDER TO HEAL

There is a well-known Rwandan proverb that says: "The days are strung together, but none is the same." No day is the same; every day brings something new.
That day in 1998 seemed just like any other ordinary day, as the day before and probably the day after would look the same.
I was still working at CESTRAR and made my way to my office in Kigali, greeted my colleagues, had a quick chat and went to my counter to prepare myself for my work and for the clients who would be coming along that day. The morning passed by. At my counter it was quiet and I had some time to catch up with some administrative tasks.
Almost inaudibly, the door was pushed open and someone came walking into the office who I then heard carefully shuffling over to my counter. The footsteps fell silent. I looked up to see who it was… and my eyes looked straight into the eyes of my former neighbour, Mukansanga, the mother of Manasse! MANASSE! The man who had murdered my children! Mukansanga stood before me clutching an envelope tightly in her hand. My heart stopped. For a moment I stared at her, stunned. Then I jumped up, flinched backwards and went crazy. I started to scream, to shout: "There! Look there! Mukansanga! What is she doing here? She must have come to find out where I am so that her son can come and kill me, just like he killed my children!" Indignation and rage welled up inside me and seized control.

Mukansanga cowered and pressed the envelope even more tightly to her. She fixed me with a helpless look and then suddenly started sobbing. In a high voice, she cried: "No! No, Beata, I have come to ask for your forgiveness. I never thought that my son was capable of such things, that he was capable of killing people. He sent me with this letter in which he expresses his remorse. He feels remorse for his actions... asks for your forgiveness."

She choked on the words. An uncomfortable silence fell. We heard nothing but Mukansanga's sobbing. My colleagues and the few clients looked at me and at the woman, shocked. Since I was so upset, one of my colleagues stepped forward, took the envelope from Mukansanga's hands and opened it. His eyes scanned the letter and he suddenly called out: "This letter has come from prison! It is dated January 31st 1998."

He quickly began to take in the contents of the letter. Then he looked at me again and said aloud: "He expresses remorse... he admits the murders... asks for forgiveness." Then he began to read aloud:

To the Prosecutor of the Republic in Gitarama,
Written with the approval of the director of the prison in Gitarama.

Sir Prosecutor,
Having read Law No. 8/98 of August 30th 1996, articles 4 to 16, I have decided to ask my country and the families who have lost their loved ones for forgiveness for my bad behaviour and my despicable murders.
I committed the first murder at eight o'clock on April 19th in Nkinda, in the Mpanga sector belonging to the Kijoma commune. Our leader was Kanamugire Elie, president of the MRND political party in the Remera sector, who was present with several police officers in his car.
This group, to which I belonged, killed:
1. Maruveri, who was shot dead by the gendarmes.
2. Theogene, a young man who was beaten to death with a nailed club.

3. Many more Tutsis whose names I cannot now remember. While there were so many people killing, I do remember the names of the murderers Nshokeye, Straton and Cyamatare who arrived in an open pick-up, together with another large group of murderers. One of the victims, Mugarura, escaped and so he saw us about our business; you can ask him about it all.

The second killing spree in which I was involved that same day, took place between ten and eleven o'clock. The murderers received a signal to go to Nyakabuye under the command of a certain Hashim. We searched everywhere - forests, banana plantations, sorghum fields - for Tutsis. We also searched Hutu houses because the Tutsi houses had already been burned down or destroyed.

We took the following people prisoner and then killed them:
1. *Gakeri's daughter-in-law and two grandchildren.*
2. *Gashongore.*
3. *Rwatamanywa's wife.*
4. *Aloys' entire family.*
5. *Rutembesa's entire family.*
6. *Others, whose names I no longer remember.*

We used clubs and small pickaxes to break their skulls. Apolinarie is the only Tutsi who was able to escape this massacre.

Regarding the third killing spree, I don't remember the date exactly, but it was after April 23rd. At nine o'clock I proceeded to the checkpoint by Centre Progrès. There I came into contact with the soldier Bapfakurera, nicknamed Muzuwi, with two of Cyamatare's brothers and also with Celestin and Mivumbi.

We killed Ntabwoba, his wife and his daughter, two of Rucyahana Placide's daughters and many Tutsis who we had picked up from their hiding places. Among them I saw a lot of old people, but there were also many young children.

Speciose saw us. The killing on that day was led by Nzigiyimfura Vincent and his brothers.

Many Tutsis were killed on that day. They were from our region, but also from other regions. They had tried to hide in and around the forest or in the bushes. The number of victims was much higher than 120. I personally killed 38 people that day.

The fourth killing spree took place on April 28th at around ten o'clock, after a heavy rainstorm. An Elektrogaz vehicle came along, transporting military. The soldiers had taken three Tutsis prisoner, namely Kayonga, Gasubiliza and Damien. I also had two with me, namely Kimonyo and his brother Rwabitenga. The soldiers gave us the order to kill them all. We made the five of them lie down on the ground and we began beating them with nailed clubs. Noticing that Kayonga had not yet died, I threw a big rock on his chest, which finished him off.
As far as Gasubiliza is concerned, he was not dead either so I beat his brains in with a pickaxe and so put an end to his life. Rwabitenga and his brother were killed by Nabasanzino from Kibuye, and by Sabagilirwa Elias.
My neighbour Jeanette saw us and everything that we did.

Sir Prosecutor,
Through that which I have just written to you, I feel deep within my heart that I have committed unspeakable crimes, which no man can imagine. I am sorry for this and I assure you that, if I am ever forgiven, I will never do anything like this ever again and from this moment on will respect every human being.
I thank you. Peace be with you.

Signed,
Nshimyerugira Manasse

The uneasy silence resumed. You could feel, no, you could hear everyone thinking. My colleague lowered the letter and we looked at each other, trying to gauge a reaction in each other's eyes to what had been read out. Manasse's mother was shaking, trembling, as she looked at us awaiting a reaction.
The contents of the letter sank in slowly and I suddenly felt my self-control return.
"Go away, Mukansanga! I know your low, mean tricks only too well, your ruthless butchery! Your child is in prison, but mine…? Mine are all dead. You can still visit your son; I will never see

my children again. Go to hell! Get out of my sight, before I do something!" I shouted angrily. Mukansanga shuffled to the door, stammered good day, but nobody felt her worthy of a look.

She'd barely left the office when everyone started moving again and started to chatter away, commenting on what Manasse had written. Some colleagues reacted indignantly and wondered what the intention of the letter was. Manasse had done so much evil, had murdered so many people and had also destroyed the lives of the survivors. What person could possibly forgive so much evil?

Forgive! Forgive? Forgiveness? I personally couldn't hear the word forgiveness anymore. I often recited The Lord's Prayer, the prayer that Jesus taught to his disciples and in which you can find the following words: "Forgive us our trespasses, as we forgive those who trespass against us." Yes, even though I had recited The Lord's Prayer a hundred times, I hadn't managed to absorb - or I didn't want to absorb - exactly what I was praying: "... as we forgive those who trespass against us..."

I immediately walked away when someone started talking about forgiveness: "Hutus! I forgave them in 1959, in 1963, in 1973 and even again in 1990. But now, after the genocide, I can't anymore. I can't and I don't want to!"

When I arrived home in the evening, embittered and full of hatred, I put Manasse's letter to one side and left it for what it was. Try to quickly forget it! Don't think about it anymore! At least, that was my intention, but that just isn't human nature, or my nature, it would seem. The letter had had a greater effect than I'd suspected. Manasse and his letter remained uninvited inside my head. Even so, the contents of the letter occupied my thoughts more and more, and began to influence my life in an overwhelmingly gloomy way.

In my imagination I saw Manasse killing Tutsis. I saw him throwing stones at the victims' heads, at their chests, aiming for the heart in order to gruesomely take their lives. I heard the voices of the innocent victims in their agony and especially the screaming of the children. Terrible images that constantly resurfaced.

Time and time again images of the numerous killings that Manasse had described played in my head. It became an obsession. When I wanted to go to sleep in the evening, the letter appeared in my mind, causing me great discomfort as I visualized all the atrocities that Manasse had committed. Manasse fixed himself in my soul; he held my mind hostage, controlled my thoughts and my life, wherever I was or whatever I was doing. Any time of the day, yes, I can honestly say twenty-four hours a day, he determined the rhythm of my existence and of my thoughts. I could no longer escape!
Would I ever be rid of these obsessive feelings? Or had I to spend the rest of my life condemned to this obsession with Manasse?

Two years later, in 2000, a second letter followed. A letter for me, but my neighbour Mugabowishema also received one. Just like me, he had survived the genocide and had lost nearly all of his family members, all killed by Manasse, who had, as he had already confessed in his first letter, murdered many people.
Again Manasse expressed his remorse and again he asked for forgiveness. I consciously read the letter to myself and then reread it. Word for word, line for line. As I contemplated it, I allowed the contents to sink in. Besides the deep feelings of revulsion that this letter incited, I realised more and more that I couldn't continue to live my life in this way. I began to see ever more clearly that I really had to put an end to my tolerance of these negative thoughts, caused by Manasse and his crimes. I had to stop tormenting myself by allowing him to constantly occupy my thoughts. I had to stop myself from judging him in my head, seeking vengeance, constantly playing the role of victim of his criminal behaviour. The whole day through, those morose, painful memories kept bubbling to the surface whenever I thought about Manasse. In those moments intense anger rose within me once again and I felt an overwhelming sense of sorrow. I felt feelings of vengeance towards him, pity for myself and injustice over everything that had happened to me six years ago. I became ever more conscious of the fact that there was only

one way to get Manasse out of my head, to give my damaged existence a reason, and to make my life liveable again.

I would have to forgive him. I HAD TO FORGIVE MANASSE! Show him mercy for everything that he had done to me and my family. Only then would I be able to free myself from the rampant negativity that was presently ruling my life.

I compare it to the sting of the 'umuyugiri', an African bee which leaves its stinger behind in the skin. If you run after the bee angrily, you hang onto the pain. Only by removing the stinger will you eventually be relieved of the pain. Manasse was the bee that had stung me; his deeds were the stinger that was causing me so much pain. I was busy running after Manasse, but had neglected to remove the stinger.

I consciously resolved to approach Manasse and his appalling crimes in a different way. First, I had to learn to banish him from my thoughts and to give myself the chance to build up a hopeful existence with new and stronger vitality.

In order to achieve this, I could not keep looking back in pain and resentment. I realised only too well that, because of my choice, not only did the most difficult path lay ahead of me, but also a very long one, a very tough task.

To forgive, to let go, these thoughts seem so simple but the reality is far from simple. Forgiveness requires emotion. Emotion that had been embodied in all those painful memories and feelings anchored in my heart and my body, causing me physical suffering. Forgiveness does not mean forgetting the appalling events that we all experienced! Never ever can or will I forget the murders committed upon my family, on us Tutsis. I will cherish the memory of my lost loved ones until the day I die. Forgiveness doesn't erase the crime, doesn't nullify the administration of justice and doesn't revoke the sentence.

For me personally, forgiveness involves several important aspects. I must keep the past alive within me by continuing to commemorate it. At the same time this includes recognition of the evil that our neighbours have done unto us.

In spite of all the horrors that I experienced, I understand that stubbornly holding onto the past or onto painful sorrow offers no prospects.

It goes against all of my feelings but I will have to accept that what has been done has been done and cannot be undone. That also requires the ability to look ahead to tomorrow and build on hopeful and positive prospects.

Forgiveness requires courage. It means that I dare to sail against the mutinous winds of sorrow and anger, by constantly reflecting consciously that I am prepared to change. And that includes: sincerely accepting expressions of remorse from the wrongdoer. There are plenty of widows who don't understand how I can think and talk about forgiveness.

"How can you forgive such a bastard? What hasn't he done to you and me? You have no right to talk to me about forgiveness, let alone force it upon me!"

"Don't talk to me about those guys!" say the girls who were raped and infected with HIV. Because every time, every day when they have to take their medication, those unbearable memories come back to the surface.

I know a girl who doesn't want to forgive her rapists. She stopped washing herself, her clothes too, so that the rapists could see exactly what they had done to her. She walked around sick, unkempt. If I took her aside and began speaking of forgiveness, she became angry: "Maybe you should go to the prison and let those guys there ask for forgiveness!" she said. She is only slowly climbing out of that vale. I expect that there will come a day when she will be able to forgive them because she is more concerned about her future now.

In my experience, forgiveness has a therapeutic and beneficial influence and has cured me of hateful feelings. Forgiveness helped me to temper the disquiet deep within me. It purifies, and it put me in a state where I could focus on tomorrow.

Now I concentrate less on the past that previously dominated my life, from first thing in the morning until last thing at night. I no longer think of revenge, but of suppressing evil thoughts by allowing myself to be led by such positive elements as faith and hope.

Forgiveness is a mysterious power, which is difficult to describe. It liberated me in any case from a heavy burden. I no longer need to obsessively occupy myself with all of Manasse's misdeeds. 'Distancing myself' is my new goal.

Of course I realise only too well that Manasse killed my loved ones and my dear friends. But nevertheless I am forced to clear the way, to strive for a more conscious future.

From all of those considerations, from all the discussions with other survivors, there grew inside me the need to help others, to put myself at the service of people that needed help.

The best way to begin was by bringing up my three children and four orphaned children of my brother and sister, who lived with me after the end of the genocide. I had to ensure that they had a good and hopeful future, and encourage them to do the best for themselves, for Rwanda and, if possible, for the whole world.

As far as Manasse's letters were concerned, they ensured that we were able to discover the names of the other genocidaires who, along with Manasse, committed so many murders. They provided clues and so enabled us to locate the places where our beloved family members had been murdered. We were able to dig up their bodies, which had been lying hidden in pits or in the forests, and bury them again with all appropriate honours due to our loved ones.

The letters proved their value in the gacaca hearings of 2006, 2007 and 2008, especially in those prosecutions where some of the genocidaires denied their crimes.

On January 28th, 2008 I received another letter from genocidaire Martin Tubanankenga, a miscreant who has a number of criminal activities on his conscience.

In his letter he named genocidaires who had killed many Tutsis in Nyanza and the Remera sector, including my two daughters Claudette and Joyeuse. He was able to say where and with whom they met up and made plans for the genocide. It seemed obvious to us now that the biggest miscreants among them were Jean Damascene Dirimasi and his brothers-in-law Placide Kabanda, Paul Ukobizaba and Joseph (Bwanamudogo) Ukobizaba, all intellectuals. Martin spoke of the twenty-nine most important leaders of the massacres in the sector. I noticed that Martin didn't mention a word about his own part in the massacres during the genocide.

I can't forget a third letter in 2002, which came from a young man Sindayigaya, who had been ten years old in 1994. Hutus did not shy away from getting small children to take part 'in the hunt'. These boys were used as scouts to track Tutsis. It is almost unimaginable, but I was told that even a boy of ten had killed people with a machete.

Sindayigaya had been part of the group that had looted everything from my house. He confessed that he had stolen my four chickens. In addition, he had taken a mattress and some of my children's clothing. Could I forgive him for stealing from me, he asked me full of remorse. He thanked me at the same time for the food, the milk and the field work that I had often offered his mother. Later, on December 13th, 2006, when I met him at the gacaca, he entrusted me with the names of those who had killed and eaten my cows and confessed that his older brother and he had taken kilos of meat home. He also told me that his uncle Sabagilirwa was one of the group of leaders who had made lists of the people to be killed.

The boy was straightforward and honestly admitted that he was one of the looters. He acknowledged his ill deeds and asked me from the depths of his heart for forgiveness. He was so sorry that he let his tears flow freely. When he walked past our destroyed house, the trauma resurfaced and he thought about my murdered family, about my children with whom he had enjoyed playing, about the milk and the banana juice that his mother had brought for him after she had worked for us.

I forgave him and told him that he didn't need to compensate me for what he had destroyed. My pardon was an honest one, came straight from my heart and was unconditional. True forgiveness is unconditional.

People who believe in Jesus Christ know that his last words on the cross were: "Father, forgive them for they know not what they do." He forgave those who crucified him and those who condemned him to his crucifixion.

In the Bible (Matthew 18), the disciples ask Jesus: "Lord, how many times shall I forgive my brother or sister who sins against me? Up to seven times?" Jesus, who understands the important value of forgiveness, answers: "I tell you, not seven times, but seventy times seven!"

And so we should follow His good example. We should follow Him by forgiving others. The Holy Ghost gave me the strength to walk this difficult path and to accept my cross.

Asking for and granting forgiveness are two essential conditions of being able to continue to live together, but maybe also the hardest to realise. They require people to conquer their inner resistance, caused by resentment or shame. Asking for forgiveness, and forgiving, must come from the heart. When honestly and sincerely meant, this will have a positive effect on the mind.

Looking back I note that learning to forgive is an organic process and requires a certain amount of time. It cost me six stressful years, during which I evolved step by step, to the point where I was able to pardon the guilty without reservation.

Six long years, with the help of others and… by sharing a lot with others. You need those others, I'm convinced of that. You can't do it alone. This is especially true for people who lost all their family during the genocide, for people who are traumatised and are alone, and who run the risk of not being able to cope with life anymore. For them, help and guidance are vitally important. Now that I've conquered the greatest obstacles on the road to forgiveness, I think back in appreciation of all those who helped me during that period. I think about the lessons of pastor Antoine Rutayisire during the reflective meetings of the Jehova Sharom prayer group, later known as Sharom Ministries, with Drocella, the woman who had brought me into contact with Jean Gakwandi and Solace Ministries, as co-ordinator.

I also think of the meetings with the group of widows. Every first Saturday of the month we met under the name Eben-Ezer (He who is our guide). There I met, among others, Agnes, Jeanne, Denise, Asterie, Seraphine, Colette and Rosa Mukamusana, the co-ordinator. In open conversations we exchanged our intense thoughts and sought a realistic way to implement forgiveness. As the thirsty long for water, so we longed for the word of God and were extremely curious as to what the Bible's scriptures had to say on the issue of forgiveness.

I dare to say openly and honestly: forgiveness is a personal process that grows from within. It develops from within your heart. Nobody can impose it upon you or force you to do it. Forgiveness heals people, in my experience.

Forgiveness banishes fear; forgiveness illuminates the memory and thought. Forgiveness gives you the courage to think about tomorrow and not only the past and the perpetrators.

And more importantly, forgiveness brings hope into your life.

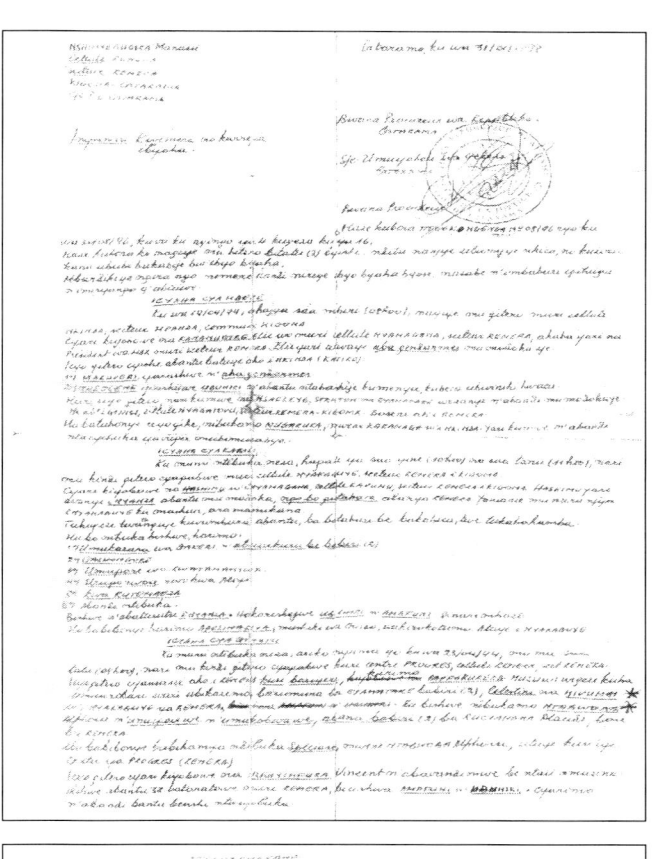

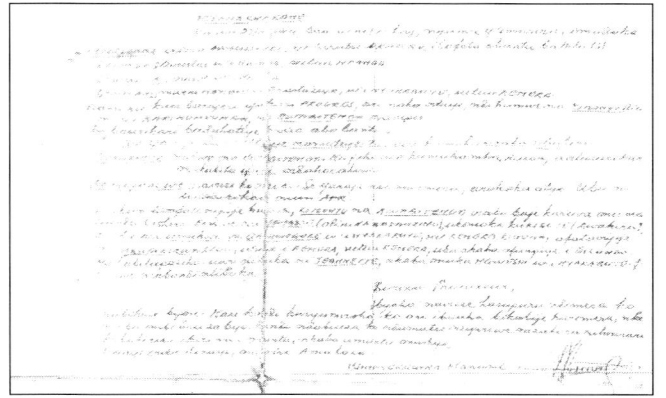

The first letter of Manasse Nshimyerugira, from 1998, in which he asks for forgiveness for the murder of two of my children.

*The second letter of Manasse, from 2000,
in which he asks me for forgiveness.*

My husband Placide: 'To forgive is not to forget.'

WITNESS FOR THE GACACA

People had seated themselves on the grass; men in light shirts and women with coloured headscarves. Young children sat among them, some pressing themselves against their mothers. One or two had erected a parasol to protect themselves from the sun; others sought the shade of bushes or a tree. Most sat on the ground, however.

A modest wind caressed the grass, bringing hair and clothing gently in motion. The soft breeze rustled slowly upwards and caused the branches and leaves of the surrounding trees and bushes to gently sway.

A muffled buzzing filled the air above the open terrain, as the wind inhaled the many voices only to exhale them out over the hills.

At first it seemed relaxed, but there was an undertone of hope and expectation in the buzzing of the voices, second-guessing the verdicts and the kind of justice that would prevail. There was also sorrow and pain, anger and resentment.

More people arrived, looking for family or acquaintances, acknowledging and greeting each other. They joined, or remained standing behind those sitting, in anticipation of what was to come. An observant spectator could have picked out various faces of people who were not aware of what was going on around them. Those introspective people heard and saw the atrocities before them over again.

Now and then loud, rough voices came from the crowd. A child began to cry.
Suddenly, the murmur of voices died down and all eyes looked ahead, full of expectation. There was a nervous tension in the air. All attention was focused on a long table with nine chairs behind it, that had been set up in front of the 'centre de conseil'. Men in pink prison uniforms were brought onto the terrain under police escort and were seated to the right of the table. On the other side, to the left of the table, I took my place.

"The days are strung together, but none is the same." I have already quoted this Rwandan expression. No, no day is the same. You just have to wait and see what the new day brings.
The day I received the summons from the court, I was really disconcerted and reminded of those words. The days of the gacaca disrupted the usual everyday rhythm of my life. The idea of seeing the murderers again and confronting them face to face evoked so much emotion and tension in me. The trials made such an impression on me that I will never forget them!
Gacaca! Before the genocide I had already heard of gacaca, a sort of tribunal before which you had to appear if you were suspected or accused of a crime. But also if the authorities needed further information in a lawsuit. The 'Exécutif' then sent a 'convocation', a summons.
The gacaca, or people's court, formed a unique legal system in our history that had come from the community itself, and in which wise men or village elders pronounced verdicts on conflicts in their own village.
In Rwanda, after the genocide, there were an untold number of suspects locked away in the overcrowded prisons, but there was a severe shortage of qualified and professional judges because many of them had been murdered during the genocide or had fled the country. For the Rwandan government it was impractical to bring all of these defendants before court, because the trials would take dozens of years - maybe even one hundred years. That is why the government resurrected the gacaca, whereby

important people with integrity from the surrounding area were appointed judges. Often, judges were among the more highly educated, or were wise elders. In total, some 12,000 gacaca tribunals operated, spread throughout the whole country.

Suspects were separated into categories depending on the type of crime that they were alleged to have committed. Under category 1, or the most serious crimes, were the crimes of planning genocide and rape. Category 2 crimes included murder and physical assault. Looters belonged to category 3.

Category 2 and 3 defendants appeared before the gacaca tribunals, while category 1 defendants were originally required to appear before formal courts. But because it would have taken more time than originally estimated for the regular courts to try all those charged with sexual violence, the Rwandan government decided in 2008 to allow the gacaca tribunals to prosecute those category 1 defendants as well. Special precautionary measures were taken to prevent defendants or their families from threatening or intimidating the survivors of these crimes.

The establishment of the gacaca tribunals allowed the possibility of attaining relatively swift justice for the victims, who testifed in front of the court, and the defendants. There was an additional advantage to the re-implementation of the gacaca: many suspects could be tried and convicted within a relatively short period of time.

This alternative way of administering justice allowed the state to promote a sense of fairness, by which the many who had suffered so deeply under the murderous terror of the genocide felt that there had at least been some reparation. Eventually, in the space of around ten years, approximately one million suspects were tried via the gacaca system. The last gacaca trial was officially held in 2012.

I also received a 'convocation' - dated December 13th, 2006 - to testify before the gacaca against Manasse Nshimyerugira, accused of complicity in the murder of my children and neighbours. I was required to appear before the gacaca on December 20th at eight o'clock in the morning at the specified place in Nyanza.

It was with mixed feelings that I read the convocation and I felt doubt growing inside me. Should I accept the invitation or not? After a lot of deliberation, I eventually decided that I would not go. No, I didn't have any need for it. But I did want to send along those letters that Manasse and Martin had written me. In that way, I could do my bit and provide the judges with enough evidence to convict Manasse.

I called my friends Drocella, Denise and Rose: "Pray for me! I have received a convocation to appear before the gacaca." During the telephone conversation I informed them that I wasn't planning on appearing before the gacaca.

Denise immediately objected and didn't think that was a good idea. She tried to persuade me to appear at this important session. At the end of the conversation, she reminded me of the great value of justice and the importance of that trial for me. In support of her words of encouragement on the telephone, she sent me a letter with text from Ezekiel, chapter 3, verses 8 and 9: "But I will make you as unyielding and hardened as they are. I will make your forehead like the hardest stone, harder than flint. Do not be afraid of them or terrified by them, though they are a rebellious people."

Yes, these words gave me assurance because the strength of God would support me in my testimony. So I decided to comply with the convocation from the gacaca. My decision was final. Yes, now I was convinced: I would go and I awaited the appointed day in anticipation.

That December 20th, I left Kigali early together with Sophie and Clementine, two orphans whose parents had also been killed by Manasse. Nervousness and tension travelled with us. On the way, we prepared ourselves for the session and exchanged thoughts on how best to compose ourselves in front of the murderers.

We arrived in Nyanza, the place where the hearing was to take place, and we made our way straight to the grounds where the gacaca, the Mpanga tribunal of our Remera sector, awaited us at eight o'clock.

A long table was set up before about two hundred members of the public, who had been called to this gacaca either verbally or by way of the many posters.

I recognised a lot of residents of the former district of Remera, but I also saw people who I didn't know. There were probably also people who were possible witnesses, who had lived in the area where the massacres took place.

I did notice that a great number of Manasse's family members were present, that is to say his parents, brothers and sisters, aunts and uncles, and nephews and nieces.

I sat on the left of the court amidst Sophie, Clementine and seven others, all victims or witnesses of Manasse's crimes.

On the right hand side of the court sat three men - genocidaires, and among them Manasse - dressed in pink prison uniforms. Two would serve as witnesses.

The nine judges, wearing a sash in the colours of the new Rwanda (blue, yellow and green), took their seats behind the big table.

The president of the court stood up. The buzzing subsided and stopped completely when he began to speak. Everyone listened attentively to his words. He started by stating that his first task as chairman was to explain the proceedings of the gacaca to the attendees.

"We will begin by observing a one minute silence to commemorate the victims who were killed. Then the trial will begin. The accused will come forward, hold up his right hand and swear that he will speak the truth and accept that he understands the consequences of telling lies. You may only say something if this is requested or permitted by the judges. It is strictly forbidden to interrupt the speaker. Nobody will laugh, shout or call out; the hearing will take place peacefully. The survivor must feel comfortable and has the right to speak in order to give testimony or to ask for information about the death of his or her family."

And so the judge continued with his introduction.

When the procedure had been explained, the president requested that those present stand in order to pay their respects in a dignified way to all victims of the genocide by observing a minute's silence. It was silent. After this impressive ceremony, everyone sat down again.

The president opened the hearing and called the name Manasse Nshimyerugira. He stood up, came forward and stood in front of the court and those present. He held up his hand and followed the regulations, as imposed by the president.

Already during the judge's introduction, Clementine, Sophie and I looked at each other without saying a word. We nervously awaited what Manasse would say and what he would confess.

He began his confession by giving testimony of his murders and admitted them unequivocally. And so the murders of my children and of the families of Clementine and Sophie were brought up and he again admitted that he was guilty of their deaths. He was also willing to explain why he had committed these crimes. Under pressure from the mayor and egged on by other prominent villagers, he had allowed himself to be persuaded to take part in the daily hunt for Tutsis and to get so carried away that he actively participated in killing a lot of people.

In tears he expressed remorse in the name of the Republic of Rwanda but also for himself, and asked for forgiveness from all the relatives of those killed. After his testimony, Manasse was shown back to his place.

One of the judges asked whether someone wanted to respond to the words of the defendant.

I had brought with me the letters that Manasse had written me to compare his words with the statement that he had made here before the court. His words before the court and those in the letter coincided, so I didn't take the judge up on his offer.

Then the president announced that it was the turn of us survivors to speak.

I was overcome by doubt. What could I do? Did I dare to testify here or should I just hand over the letters?

"Oh God, God!" I prayed deep from my heart and kept repeating: "Fill me with wisdom and strength, give me courage, You who know all truth, who knows what happened and whose judgement is fair."

The judge called my name. I stood up. I was very nervous. All eyes were now on me, including those of Manasse and his family. "Oh God, stand by me!"

My heart beating like a drum, I walked to the front and handed the two letters from Manasse over to the president. I explained how they had come into my possession and that Manasse had admitted the murders in those letters. I also mentioned that I had put the first letter to one side, but that the second letter had set me thinking. The judges decided to read aloud the two letters so that the contents were also known to all present.

When I spoke again, I felt more confident.

"I accept your expression of remorse and I forgive you, Manasse. I appreciate that you have confessed and have shared with us the names of all the people that you killed, that you have indicated the places where the bodies lie, and that you have named the complicit genocidaires. But Manasse, you haven't told me where I can find the body of my husband, Placide."

I knew by now that Placide had been killed on April 24th. Witnesses had seen him, together with a number of others, loaded onto a blue pick-up that day in Nyanza and driven out of the village. That vehicle had last been spotted at the nearby lake. After that the trail runs cold and nobody knows what happened next.

Manasse claimed in front of the judges, however, that he knew absolutely nothing about the death of Placide. I heard him deny it explicitly. But could I believe him? Could I trust him? Because Manasse, neither in your letter nor here in front of the judges, have you made any mention of the rape of women and young girls that you have on your conscience. Because truth be told, everyone has been waiting for that confession from you! But you have remained silent on that matter.

I resumed my seat and Clementine and Sophie spoke.

First of all, Sophie wanted to know from Manasse where he and his accomplices had left the bodies of her father, my husband and Clementine's father. Manasse was unable to give an answer, he said, because after the massacre he had left immediately to go and slaughter a cow with which he had been rewarded for his part in the killing. When he had left, those named were most probably still alive and had been transported elsewhere to be murdered later.

Unbelievable! Some had to walk for miles first before they were killed. Why, in heaven's name?

In the two letters, there was no mention at all of the death of my husband Placide, of Mwumvaneza, Sophie's father, of Gafiligi, Clementine's father, and many others, the majority of whom were teachers, businessmen, students and the elderly.

One of the judges again urged Manasse to disclose more names of the perpetrators who he had murdered with. He named them and one of the other judges noted precisely what he had confessed.

In their turn, the other survivors delivered their valuable contribution by adding what they knew about Manasse and his crimes, and they also asked him questions to learn more about their disappeared family members. Finally, the other two prisoners informed the judges and those in attendance about what they knew of Manasse's crimes.

After all the witness statements, the president closed the hearing and announced the date upon which the verdict would be delivered.

Everyone left the grounds and we took a taxi back to Kigali.

On the day of the verdict, we returned to Nyanza. The court sentenced Manasse to thirty years in prison because he (and his accomplices) had been found guilty of many murders committed in April, May and June of 1994. Although Manasse had confessed to a lot of murders, he had not admitted to them all.

The gacaca hearings in Mpanga went on for a while and we visited every last one of them. Sometimes we were happy with the outcome, but other times we were left with a less positive feeling, especially when the killers refused to say where they had dumped or buried the bodies of the victims. To this very day, I have not been able to find my husband or the others who were killed with him. I have not been able to give Placide a final resting place. The genocidaires still refuse to reveal where they dumped the bodies.

By no means did all genocidaires make use of the opportunity to confess their crimes and ask for forgiveness, even though the gacaca expressly offered the opportunity to do this. Since justice was being administered there, it could have also been a venue to begin reconciliation and forgiveness.

But no, they continued to deny their crimes, demonstrated their insincerity and dishonesty, and waived their right to reconcile with the survivors. During the hearings in Mpanga, not a single genocidaire confessed to rape, either verbally or in writing.

In 2005 I visited the prison in Nyanza with four female survivors in an attempt to find out more about where the bodies of our loved ones, such as my husband Placide, had been left. But none of the genocidaires involved gave us an answer.

During an international conference on international crimes in 2013, I again visited the Mpanga prison in Nyanza together with all the other conference participants to speak to Manasse and other perpetrators. Manasse then informed me about his accomplices and repeatedly asked for forgiveness for the murders. Even the other genocidaires admitted they'd been wrong, expressed their remorse and asked for forgiveness. Concerning the place where Placide's body had been dumped, neither Manasse nor the other killers could give me any information. He did promise, though, that were he to find out anything about my husband, he would let me know.

When I look back on the gacaca system that was reintroduced after the genocide, I conclude that it had its advantages and its disadvantages:

Advantages include:
- Survivors learned the names of other murderers, who they had not known about before. In addition, locations of the bodies of victims were revealed, such as latrines and pits.
- Genocidaires who confessed their crimes before the court gave the survivors the chance to grant forgiveness. A small number of genocidaires asked the survivors for forgiveness, and in some cases there was a kind of reconciliation.
- The gacaca worked faster than the regular courts. The latter would have required tens of years to process all of the genocide cases.
- Gacaca tribunals were held in places where the perpetrators committed their crimes, so the local community could take part in the trials.
- The gacaca trials had a healing influence on the assimilation of the great suffering caused by the genocide and all the problems resulting from it for Rwandans.
- Sexual violence, which was systematically committed during the genocide, was unconditionally recognised as one of the most serious of crimes and severely punished.

But there are also negative aspects to report:
- It was traumatic for victims to hear a number of genocidaires continue to deny their role in murders, which survivors had witnessed with their own eyes.
- It was a traumatic experience for survivors to hear the details of the perpetrators' cruelty when carrying out the murders of their family members. Some genocidaires often expressed themselves during their testimonies in coarse, crude language, without any pity, and shamelessly revealed provocative details about their torture, which severely shocked the survivors:

'Naramuhorahoje': I murdered him. He wasn't completely dead and I killed him.

'Namusize ataka': I made him scream in fear.

'Namuciye umuhogo nsiga atarahwana': I partially severed his head and neck from his body, but he wasn't completely dead, and I left him in that state.

'Abana bato twabkubitaga ku kintu bagahita bapfa ntibaturushyaga': It was easy to murder young children. We just threw them against something and they died immediately.

'Twamusize ahirita ataka asaba amazi cyangwa amata': We left him lying there in pain while he asked for water or milk.

- Gacaca judges made no pronouncements regarding compensation for physical or mental suffering, or the loss of loved ones. The genocidaires did, however, have to pay for material damages. Yet in many cases this did not happen either, because those found guilty didn't have the means. And so students who had lost both parents found themselves in financial difficulties when it came to paying tuition fees and were no longer able to finish their studies.
- Travelling to and from the gacaca hearings was expensive, especially for the poor. Because of the genocide, people had relocated, often far away from the scene of the massacres. As a result, some survivors were unable to attend the trials and testify against the accused.
- Out of fear for the high sentences for sexual violence - in principle life imprisonment - almost nobody confessed to having committed sexual violence.

Gacaca judges during the trial of Manasse, the killer of my children, at the gacaca of Mpanga in Nyanza district.

Manasse (second right) and Paul Ukobizaba (right) and other accomplices at the gacaca of Mpanga in Nyanza district.

MY LIFE AND WORK AS A TRAUMA COUNSELLOR

An ordinary sunny Wednesday morning in Kigali. From the broad boulevard, adorned with green palm trees, two women turn into a broad, bumpy sand path.
To the left, behind a heavy metal fence, four tall modern apartment buildings rise up. They radiate luxury as they glisten, soft and white. The two women walk and talk, turning the corner, and take a bumpy path that runs downwards steeply.
A big lorry roars slowly struggling towards them, leaving behind it a cloud of soot and dust. The heavy giant thunders on, and above the departing roar of the motor the rhythmic sound of singing can now be clearly heard.
A little further along, the women head down towards the big gate of Solace Ministries where the singing is coming from and reverberates ever louder. They walk into the courtyard, head for the great hall and join a colourful group of mainly women who are clapping, singing and dancing to the beat of the music. There are also a few men participating in the group.
An enthusiastic lead singer waving his arms jumps and sings brightly through the hall. His passion and his dedication draw many people up out of their seats and they accept his invitation to join the singing and dancing. A long line colours the hall and moves now, rhythmically swaying to the leader's song, chanting along in chorus, singing after him. The echo of the happy voices resounds through the hall. Boom...boom...boom! Heavy drum

beats roll through the room and their steady rhythm determines the movement. This happy looking sight is part of a trauma group session. In this way, many women are able to free themselves of their everyday reality. They are mostly women, widows, since many men were murdered during the genocide.
The song they sing urges people to thank God because He has saved them.

Ishimwe ni iryawe	*Thanks to You*
Ishimwe ni iryawe	*Thanks to You*
Ishimwe ni iryawe Yesu	*Thanks to You, Jesus*
Haleluya	*Hallelujah*
Ishimwe ni iryawe	*Thanks to You*
Ishimwe ni iryawe	*Thanks to You*
Ishimwe ni iryawe Yesu	*Thanks to You, Jesus*
Miami Mana yacu waraturinze	*Lord, our God, You protected us*
Uturinda umujinya wa Satani	*You protected us against the anger of the devil*
Uturindira muri iyi si ishaje	*You protected us in this old world*
Uraturinda ntitwapfa	*We did not die because of Your protection*
Nub twahuye n'ibigeragezo	*Even though we had to deal with sorrow*
Inzitane n'ibibazo byo mw'isi	*Conflicts and problems in this world*
Wagaragaje ukunesha kwawe	*We saw Your intervention*
Uraturinda ntitwapfa	*And You protected us from death*
Ishimwe ni iryawe	*Thanks to You*
Ishimwe ni iryawe	*Thanks to You*
Ishimwe ni iryawe Yesu	*Thanks to You, Jesus*
Haleluya	*Hallelujah*
Ishimwe ni iryawe	*Thanks to You*
Ishimwe ni iryawe	*Thanks to You*
Ishimwe ni iryawe Yesu	*Thanks to You, Jesus*

The singing and dancing continues for minutes until the women return to their seats.

The calm returns and I, who had been watching the proceedings from behind my table, come forward:

"Hallelujah!"

The women answer: "Amen!"

"HALLELUJAH!"

"Amen!"

"HALLELUJAH!"

"AMEN!"

"Praise God! Thank Him! God is our saviour."

"Amen!"

"God is great. He is our Creator. We have much to thank Him for!"

"Hallelujah."

"Amen!"

"Let us pray, let us glorify God. Let us be thankful for the life that He has given us."

"Amen."

I take my hymn book. Together we sing and clap a song.

Afterwards I ask a woman if she wants to come forward to share with us her experiences during the genocide. She bravely recounts how she was pursued by murderers. She fled, ran away with her child on her back. However, in the panic and haste, her child fell out of the baby sling to the ground. But in the anxiety of the moment nobody had noticed, not even her. The murderers caught up with her, hacked away mercilessly at her, all over her body.

She shows those present her scars: her hands are disfigured now and can only partly function.

Her story stalls for a moment. Silence. And yet she manages to summon up the strength to continue with her story. Bleeding and in a lot of pain, she went desperately looking for her child. She found it, but her hands were so badly disfigured that she was in no state to care for her child on the run. Powerless, she had to watch it die. Tears well up. Her despair and sorrow resurface as she experiences that misery again. I take her hand in mine.

The woman bravely continues. In spite of her wounds, she'd survived the genocide. However, there was no one in her family left alive. Everyone had been murdered. She was now all alone in the world. What was the point of her life now? She was, however, taken in by Solace Ministries. Here she found a new family. She thanks God for helping her and giving her existence meaning again.
"Hallelujah!"
"Amen!"

In the scene described above, the trauma group session takes place every Wednesday morning in the big hall at Solace Ministries in Kigali.
Even though the genocide is many years in the past, a lot of women are still burdened by their past experiences. For this reason, we are constantly trying to restore and inject new life into the damaged morale of these women, using words as well as music and dance, and by showing gratitude for the present day as we ask God for His help and support.
"Hallelujah!"
"Amen!"
The song quoted above, which we sing, dance and clap to, expresses our appreciation for Him. A song like that doesn't affect every person in the same way. Some widows own their sorrow in their singing and dancing; they open their hearts to the light and make themselves ever more aware that they must focus on the present and the future. Other women still remain buried in the memories of the familiar, but long lost, past and consequently find it difficult to accept the life of today and tomorrow. They are stuck in mourning for their families and cut themselves off from those who survived the genocide with them.
Of course it requires a lot of courage, perseverance and determination from the widows, as well as a lot of energy to process the terrible consequences of the genocide, energy that they need in order to carry out the tasks that each day brings, despite their often poor physical condition.

Where one person doesn't succeed, another does succeed. After years of grief, the latter can give her departed loved ones a place in her life and begin to build up hope and faith in the future again. An important prerequisite for success on the difficult path to healing and recovery is showing gratitude for life.

Also, based on my experiences, the counselling programme became the platform for our relief work at Solace Ministries and this work takes priority over our organisation's other programmes, like the material support we offer to survivors.

Because of the genocide and its extreme cruelty, many victims were left seriously traumatised. Many women were sucked into the unhallowed, dark swamp of a severely violated existence with inhuman memories. Because of this, these women still feel closer to death than connected to the living.

Our counselling programme offers therapy which focuses on encouragement and psychological healing based on individual and group therapy, in which meeting other genocide victims is key.

Our objective is to transform the depressing feeling of 'facing life alone' among our women into 'belonging' and so to give them the foundation they need in order to cope. In the security of Solace Ministries, many women find a new family.

In my work, I place emphasis on:

1. The organisation of meetings to encourage survivors to talk openly to others about what they experienced.

2. The organisation of meetings for people living with HIV and AIDS acquired through sexual violence. We offer them ample opportunity to express their suppressed anger and hatred, and to share their worries and problems with people in the same situation.

3. The organisation of weekly sessions in the local communities to promote personal development. With those who we counsel, we discuss their qualities and possibilities. We look for suitable schools for orphans and with widows, we look for possible sources of income such as in farming, manual labour or business.

On Mondays and Thursdays, we offer individual counselling for those who live in Kigali. On Tuesdays and Fridays, we plan house visits in the communities elsewhere in the country. Every first Friday of the month, we visit a large community in Nyanza. On Thursdays, we visit people in the hospital who no longer have family.

On Wednesdays, we organise group counselling, where experiences are shared, where we pray and praise God with songs and dance, and we also hear His word.

Our most important objective is to create tranquility in the minds of those where the most terrible images still remain and constantly resurface. Singing increasingly suppresses these images.

People in the group dare to stand up and speak about what they've experienced, or to disclose that they are living with HIV. In this way, they are able to help others who are not yet ready to take that step to divulge their HIV-positive status.

It took four years after the genocide for a woman to have the courage to tell the participants at the Wednesday morning session that she had been raped. After counselling from Solace Ministries, she was able to take an HIV test. Sadly, the result was positive. Thanks to our guidance and information, she began antiretroviral treatment (ARV). Now, she knows how to maintain her health, thus mitigating unpleasant side effects and secondary health issues. Her testimony signified a breakthrough for her, but also for many others, because since that day a great number of women have come forward for a preliminary chat about - voluntarily - taking an HIV test.

Solace Ministries attempts to answer participants' questions within group counselling sessions, which we organise in local communities. In these sessions, we explain to them that the God that protected them during the genocide is the same God that is watching over them now. We ask these women, many of them widows, to open themselves up to the same God. We make it clear that we gladly welcome them into our community so that they are no longer alone.

The most important aspect of counselling is listening to the person sitting before you and letting them feel your compassion, love and understanding.

A lot of people lost many or even all of their family members, meaning that they have no one close that they can express their sorrow to, or share their suffering with. Solace Ministries tries to take the place of the lost family members. In a protective, familiar environment, women share their experiences and open their hearts, airing their sorrow and suffering.

At the moment we are helping some eight thousand families across about sixty communities all over Rwanda.

I accurately keep track of all my appointments and consultations in a book. Because I find recording everything during consultations on the computer too impersonal, I have a card index and on separate cards everything is noted in detail: names, dates and subject of discussion. There must be thousands of people.

Over the years, keeping in mind the goal of appropriate counselling, we have mapped the different issues families are facing. On this basis I come to the following categories of people most deeply affected by the genocide:

- People living with HIV.
- People using antiretroviral medication.
- Single women without children, or women who have lost their husband and children.
- Women who have fallen pregnant as a result of rape.
- Young people who don't know the identity of their father.
- Couples, in which one partner is living with HIV.
- Divorced people.
- Orphaned girls, to whom we provide sex education.

From listening to many experiences in individual counselling, we discovered that many widows and girls, but also some boys, had been raped. The chance of HIV infection as a consequence of this abuse is a realistic one, and our advice to those affected is to attend a laboratory to take an HIV test, either in the hospital or at the Solace Ministries clinic. After taking the test, there follows another interview during which we evaluate the results of the test together.

A negative result is a cause for relief and can have an empowering effect. For the woman or man who tests positive, however, it comes as a hard blow. They then have the difficult task of absorbing and accepting the result. It rests on me the difficult responsibility of communicating a positive result to someone, which is especially challenging if it is a young person. You have to take a lot of time to offer them the guidance they need to face and accept the test result and its consequences.

Sometimes women think that the cause of the infection rests with them, due to their limited sexual knowledge. I consider it my duty to make clear to those women that the origin of the infection was the sexual violence that they suffered during the genocide and nothing else.

A positive result is experienced by many as quite literally a direct confrontation with death. The thought that the end is near is one that I emphatically oppose. I mention then the fact that current medication can prolong life considerably and in a dignified manner.

Time does not stand still, however, and life must go on. Especially for the younger ones: School, my studies, the future. Don't only think about death. The Solace Ministries motto is: "You are not alone, we are with you. We are here for you, to help you to get your life in order." The person concerned must first accept that the new situation they find themselves in cannot be undone and that they must be prepared to accept medical help. Only then do we proceed to the second step of making an appointment with the hospital or our clinic. There it can be determined whether it is necessary at this stage to treat the patient with medication or set out a follow-up plan for regular monitoring by a doctor or nurse.

Those who are to be treated with medication, for example in the hospital, are the first to be considered for pre-antiretroviral counselling where we provide supportive advice concerning the use of antiretrovirals. They can also avail themselves of our 'adherence counselling'; then we can also discuss the risks of transmitting the virus. But again, only if the patient has accepted and dares to face her/his condition. We go into more detail about what HIV and AIDS mean exactly: the source of the infection, the recommended treatment, how to avoid sexual transmission, and other measures to promote good health, such as good hygiene and proper nutrition.

We don't visit young people at home. In this way we prevent their neighbours from asking intrusive questions or stigmatising them due to their HIV status.

Some youth admit they are anxious about taking their medication. So I try to find a way to talk about this problem that is troubling them so much. After telling young persons about the risks that come with infection, all that remains is to allow them the opportunity, preferably through the use of open questions, to express their feelings and share why they resist taking their medication.

We give out medication as discreetly as possible, without others noticing.

I'll give an example of what can happen when an illness and the use of medication are considered taboo. A young person was once prescribed medication by a doctor and was supposed to take it every day. His mother was afraid that others would find out and for this reason she told her son that his medication was especially effective against headaches. A logical result of this was that the boy saw nothing wrong in sharing his medication with fellow students who complained of headaches. I invited mother and son to come to see me during my work hours and pointed out the consequences of her behaviour.

By talking about it together, I helped the parent and child to accept the necessity of using medication, to conquer their fear of it, and so to ultimately be honest about it.

Another important component of our programme is providing sex education to young people. Those maintaining sexual relations run the risk of becoming infected with the virus from

their partner. Abstinence is the safest way to avoid infection. If women are or wish to become pregnant, we advise them how to protect their unborn baby against the virus so that it is born without HIV.
We advise girls and women who are alone and of limited means to marry because we know from experience that a single woman is vulnerable and runs a considerable risk of ending up in prostitution. Where one partner in a couple is living with HIV and the other is not, this puts a lot of pressure on their relationship. Divorce is an easy solution, but I strongly feel it is my job to prevent this, explaining, for example, that the uninfected partner can remain safe through the use of condoms.
Family counselling is therefore also a part of my work.

Many babies were born of the genocide, the result of the widespread brutal sexual violence. Their mothers named these children 'les enfants mauvais souvenirs', or 'the children from bad memories'. For this purpose, Solace Ministries works closely with the 'Rwanda Foundation', an organisation which concerns itself with mothers who bore children as the result of a violent past.
These children pose a worrisome and complicated problem. Worrisome because these unwanted children need a normal upbringing; complicated because their fathers - known or unknown - committed a crime, namely rape.
In our conversations with these mothers, we must guarantee the utmost discretion and sensitivity, because some women are not in a position emotionally to offer their child clarity regarding their background.
We have to accept and understand that upon reaching a certain age, children are driven to find out who their father is; they want to get to know him. This often reignites the mother's trauma, certainly in cases where the mother doesn't even know who the father is. She might not know him because she was raped by several men, or because she was abused by unknown Interahamwe soldiers or by men she didn't know in another region where she had hoped to find refuge.

How do you explain to your child that his father is in prison because he murdered people? How do you make a child understand that his father - and possibly his father's family - murdered his mother's family? How can you explain that a child's mother is now infected with HIV because of the sexual misconduct of that child's father?

The tragic thing about cases like these, as I've already said, is that the father and his family murdered the mother's family. When the mother's surviving family members know this, chances are high that they then direct their anger and hatred at the child. For some mothers, this is reason enough to remain silent about the paternity of their child.

Of course, there are also mothers who just can't get over the rapes and the murders. The tragedy of their experiences has left them incapable of loving their unwanted child. With the help of counselling, we try to convince all these women, step by step, to take the responsibility to share their painful past in all honesty with their children.

Solace Ministries supports these special children in their development, for example, by paying their tuition fees. This financial help lessens the mother's worries for the child, and in some cases helps her to feel less burdened by the memories of the father's abuse.

Still, I have noticed during the counselling of these children that it is difficult to realise a positive healing process, certainly if the outside world is aware of the way the child was conceived. If, for example, one of these unwanted boys is involved in a fight at school, the other children warn each other to be careful around him, because he might just kill you, like his father. If he eats a lot, he gets mocked for eating too much, like his father, who ate all the cows. These young people often feel very unhappy and these kinds of incidents reinforce this feeling. We at Solace Ministries need to be extra vigilant about this.

Another noteworthy element is that every year in April during the commemoration of the start of the genocide, more people than usual seek psychological help. Known faces, but also new faces, sign up and we offer them guidance individually or in group sessions. We get to hear again the most terrible stories and see survivors' scars.

In cases of rape, it is easy to think only of the possibility of HIV infection but forget the violent mistreatment that women have been subjected to. Yet we also have to deal with wounds or gynaecological damage such as misformed reproductive organs that prevent many women, especially in the south of Rwanda, from menstruating on a monthly basis. There was more rape in the south of Rwanda compared with the rest of the country, and the genocide there lasted longer as well.

There were also some men raped by women. We also have a man in our practice who was castrated at a very young age by female perpetrators.

We spend a lot of time on the problems raised above, but we also try to help people in other areas. In this regard we managed to secure the services of a lawyer, on whose assistance the women can rely when legal assistance is required, for example on questions regarding possessions or land. On Wednesdays, we can avail ourselves of his expertise during working hours in Kigali.

Furthermore, we provide transport for people who have no access to transport or who are unable to travel independently, for example, to a court hearing or to a lawyer, due to frail health.

What we wish to achieve through our counselling is people who are eventually able to get on with their lives as a result of their own strength. Our objective is to support them so that they are able to look firmly towards the future rather than relive the suffering of the past. We think it's important to inspire people to continue to work on themselves and to learn to provide for themselves.

Our way of working in smaller communities results in Solace members caring for each other, through hospital visits or merely by showing compassion in special situations. If a survivor of the genocide dies, we bring their children into the Solace family. For these children it is possible to attend group therapy and to make contact with others.

We attach a lot of importance to bringing our organisation to the attention of politicians. We keep the government and politicians informed about our work and what we hope to achieve with it.
What we are grateful for is the very important support of our international partners and sponsors. They offer a welcome and essential supplement to our work and allow us the possibility to realise projects and to continue to support victims within our Solace Ministries community.

My work with Solace Ministries has always demanded a lot of time. Besides this, my three children - Dieudonné, Denise and Lambert - and the children of my brother and sister - Donatien, Eugenie, Françoise and Francine - all now in their late twenties, have always needed, and still need, my care.
Nevertheless, I still felt a strong need to complete my university studies, which I would have liked to finish when I was younger but had not been able to because of the government's attempts to legally address the 'ethnic imbalance'.
In spite of my 56 years, I decided in 2008 to complete the sixth year of high school education and I have the government to thank for making this possible. I achieved good grades in this exam and I am now a holder of the national diploma in Humanities A2 (the highest level of pre-university education).
In 2012, I began a university course in Theology with the 'Rwanda Institute of Evangelical Theology (RIET)'. I undertook these studies to lend greater depth to my work as a counsellor. Every weekday evening, I attended college after work from 5.30pm to 9pm. The courses we studied included Philosophy, History of the Church, Administration, Communication, Greek and Hebrew. I noticed during the first year that my studies were going very well, because I achieved an outstanding score of 78.5%.

On September 29th, 2015, I graduated having written my thesis on the role of Christian organisations in the lives of widows and orphans: the work of Solace Ministries (in cooperation with Mukomeze) in the Runda sector of the Kamonyi district. In order to research our work on widows and orphans, I compared our impact today in a few fundamental areas, such as health, education and income-generating activities, with a few years ago.

An orphan from Bugesera shares his testimonial with me during an individual counseling session at Solace Ministries in Kigali.

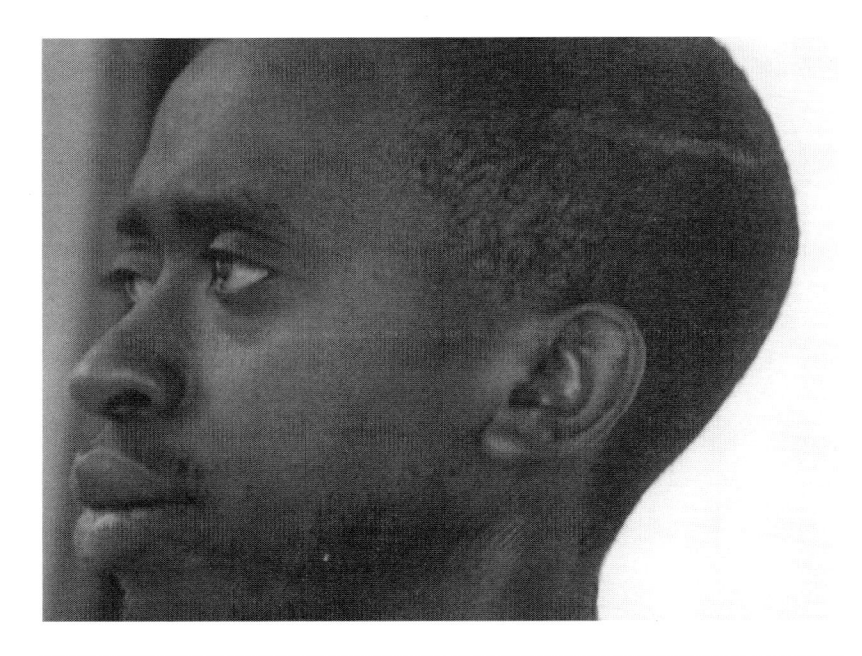

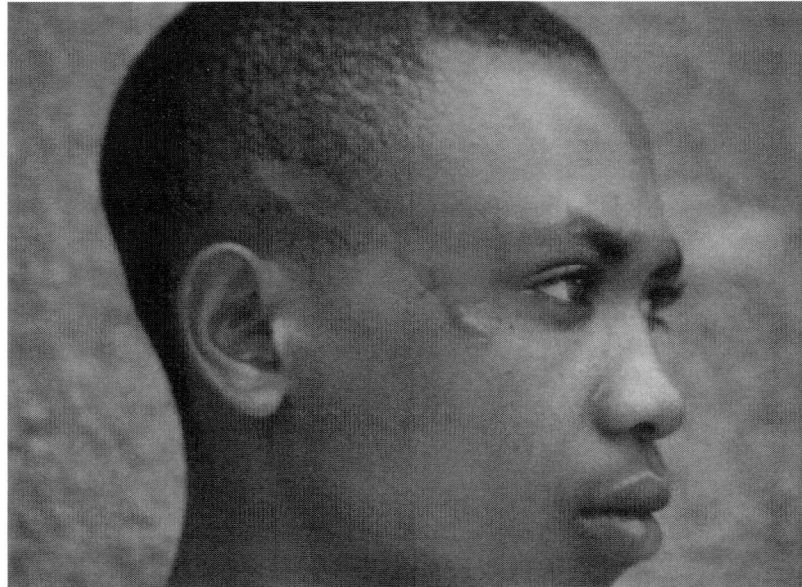

*Scarves are the visible consequences of the genocide.
Orphans whom I guide show their scarves.*

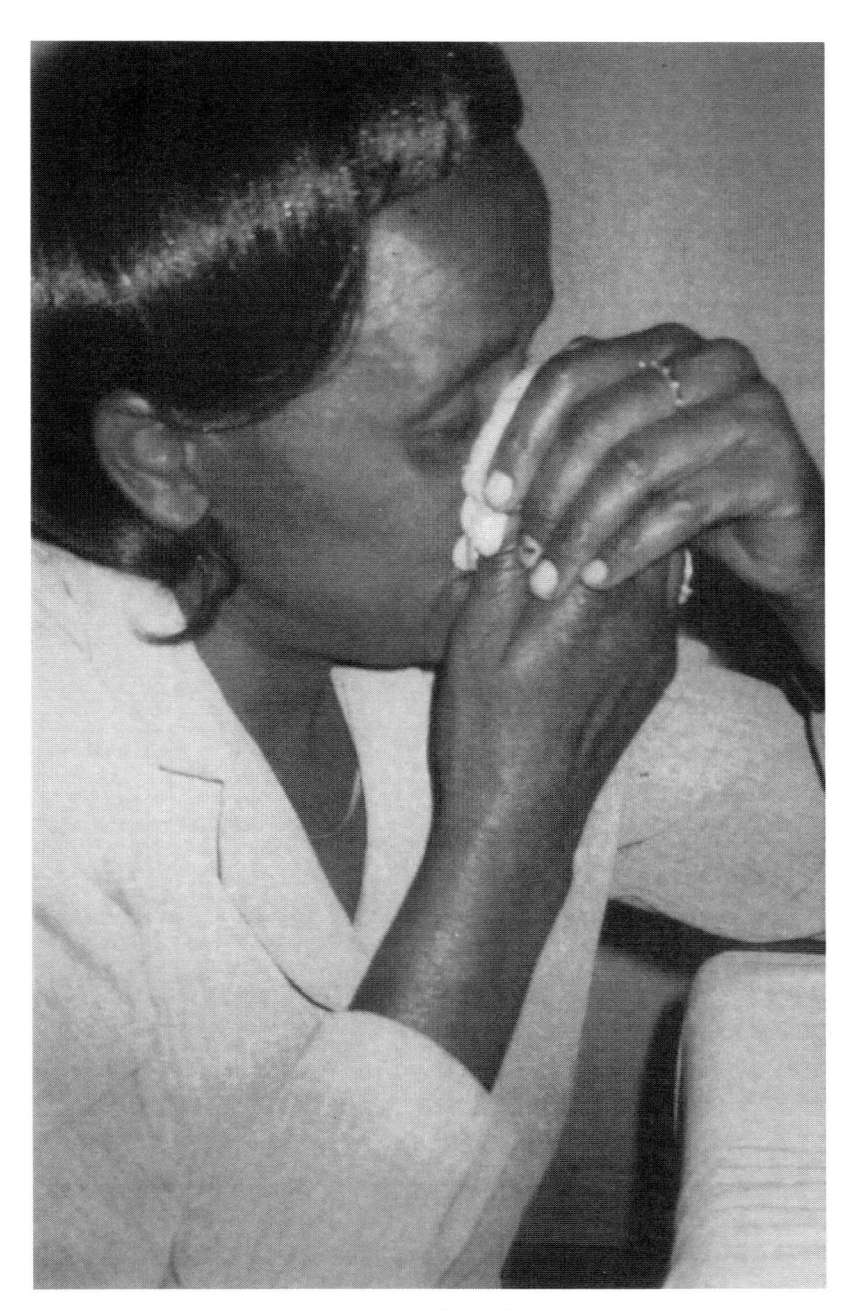

Individual counselling of a widow.

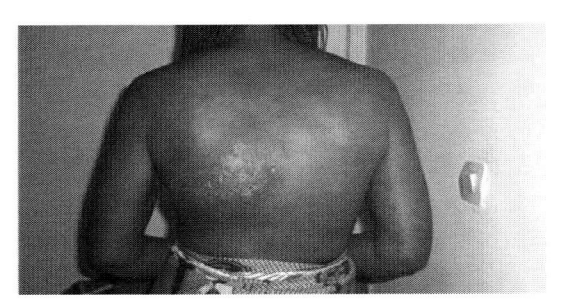

*I advise widows with HIV/AIDS.
Medication for this often provokes side-effects.
Here someone with shingles on her back.*

*Group counselling supervised by me. Emeritha mentions how she has been
strengthened by the support of Mukomeze and Solace Ministries.*

*Regularly I visit people at home to assist
and advise them.*

THE POWER OF RECONCILIATION

"I am still haunted by the events of the genocide. It astounds me still that so few people showed me compassion during that dark valley of my life. What is most sad in my life is that I see the men who raped me walk freely in Rusatira. Only two of them spent time in prison, and they are now free like the others."
Clementine Nyinawumuntu (1977)

"I don't feel that I forgive the Interahamwe, not yet. No one has asked for my forgiveness, and no one wants to talk about it. I still live among them, and the very best I can do is to ignore them."
Françoise Kayitesi (1962-2010)

"I don't think I can forgive the FAR soldiers or the Interahamwe. I don't want to hear about reconciliation. I accused them in the *gacaca* courts, including the one who raped me, those who participated in the killings in the church and those I saw at the roadblock, but now they are being released."
Marie Louise Niyobuhungiro (1975)

These three quotes can be found in the book 'The Men Who Killed Me: Rwandan Survivors of Sexual Violence' (Douglas & McIntyre 2009, pp. 116; 135; 33). They are the words of women who survived sexual violence during the genocide and sought help afterwards from Solace Ministries. They do not speak of reconciliation, but that is not much of a surprise. How do you bridge the immense chasm between victims and perpetrators? The genocide cut wounds that are so deep, that one wonders if they will ever heal.

Can we rebuild a nation on the rubble of pain and tears, blood and hatred?

Rubble that serves to remind and sustain the memory of what once happened in our country. Commemorate with monuments, commemorate with words. To keep the ones we lost alive through our tears, to renounce violence and to express, in a dignified way, the view that the blood of the many victims has not been shed in vain.

A new country with a foundation for peace and unity where being a community actually means 'living together' as Rwandans, where people respect each other as equal and full citizens and discrimination between populations is unacceptable.

A new country with a basis for reconciliation in which the offender has the courage to reach out to the survivor, pleads guilty and asks for forgiveness. Yes, in which the survivor is willing to pardon and forgive and provide real space to heal the deep breach of trust.

Only reconciliation offers hope for a better future. Several steps in this direction have already been made.

In an attempt to restore the rule of law as well as to strive for reconciliation, the Government of Rwanda reinstated gacaca courts to do justice to the victims. With the active participation of victims and witnesses, the gacaca aimed to bring perpetrators before a court, hear them, pass a fair judgment and impose an appropriate sentence. Moreover, this court gave the accused the chance to ask their victims for forgiveness for the atrocities they committed. Some perpetrators did indeed publicly apologize for their crimes. There are victims who, despite their traumatic experiences, displayed the courage to move on from their bitterness, to accept the apology and forgive the offenders. With this gesture, both parties underlined their willingness to open a common door towards the future.

Being the principal institution in the country, the government works actively in the field of reconciliation, because it is fully aware of the fact that building a future without reconciliation is not possible. In order to build bridges between perpetrators and victims and to overcome enmity, all Rwandans will have to be involved.

In the many years that I have worked with Solace Ministries, a large part of that work is dedicated to support women and orphans who are still processing the genocide. The building blocks of the support concern the themes of forgiveness and reconciliation.
When I talk about reconciliation and when I look back on my own life, I can only conclude that reconciliation is a process that requires a lot of time and, moreover, requires sacrifices.
But reconciliation is so important for every person and so necessary! Reconciliation opens the way to exchange enmity for peace. And reconciliation provides the opportunity to turn division into unity and so offer people the opportunity to live and work with each other. This certainly applies to us Rwandans, in order for us to rebuild our ruined nation.
In the end, I came to understand the vital importance of reconciliation and it started to sink in that reconciliation is the only path to a new life.
Reconcile! I have reconciled with:
… myself! I, who wanted to take my own life; I thought life was hell on earth and after all the miseries I suffered, I thought I was of no value. Now I consider myself a full human being again.
… my children. Because for a long time, I let them believe that life was completely empty. I traumatized them further, by suggesting that we had no future. What would it be without a father, without siblings, without family! What was the meaning of life post-genocide? Couldn't we just leave it behind us and get out? Now, however, I sincerely tell my children that life has meaning and encourage them to build a good future.
… my neighbours. We avoided each other, we kept to ourselves

and after the genocide we never said hello any more. Now, we talk and greet each other again.

... the killers, because I increasingly turned towards hate and resentment rather than believe in the value of life. I have forgiven and through this, have given myself a future with perspective.

... the church and all its believers, Christians in whom I had lost confidence because of the many horrible crimes from the past. I think of the churches where many people sought refuge, but where most priests hopelessly failed to provide any protection. Hutu priests killed Tutsi priests, Christians killed Christians. What values did I still have to give to the Ten Commandments?

Almost all Tutsi priests were slain during the genocide, so only Hutu priests were left to conduct services. What message did they preach? Were they sincere and honest? Did they ask for forgiveness or did they ignore the facts? I knew of priests who were detected at a barricade. I was in doubt.

I also remember very vividly the first time that I attended a church service again. It was in 1996, two years after the genocide. Before going to Communion and receiving the bread, it is customary that people embrace each other and wish each other peace. When that moment came, I felt enormous resistance inside of me! What should I do? Should or shouldn't I participate in the embrace? Do I say "Peace be with you"? Wish for peace? The peace they would not give me in 1994 - that's the peace they are suddenly wishing for me now? How can I for God's sake share peace with these people? I walked out of the church feeling failed and went home! No peace wishes!

However, this incident made me think about it all and it made me realize that it was Christ who showed us with his dead how to reconcile with God. That selfless example led me to the conviction that I had to reconcile with every human being, no matter what he had done to me! I said to myself: "Is it up to me to judge? Leave the judging to God. Let people reap for themselves what they have sown."

Paper can wait, the reality is obstinate! Besides a lot of time, this process took great effort to persevere on that self-chosen, but challenging, road. Prayer, reflection and meditation always helped me to continue to focus on my goal: reconciliation.

Several years after the genocide, I felt like I was able to open up for reconciliation without a heavy heart. It also brought deliverance. Being able to shed negative and limiting thoughts freed me from the fear of being in contact with others. I felt strong enough to think positively and freely of others and it strengthened my intention to be meaningful for that other person, to help my neighbour with all of my knowledge, effort and experience. Before, whenever I went anywhere, I always thought in the back of my mind that someone was going to kill me! Often I would be overcome by fear that would command me: Be careful! Stay in Kigali and only go where there are RPF soldiers.

In 2000, I felt ready to leave Kigali and I even had the courage to go on a trip. In the company of Drocella and Denise, both widows, I travelled, via Kampala, to Togotho, Kikuyu in Kenya. At Solace Ministries' initiative, we were sent to an Anglican conference - a revival, a healing - from which all three of us could draw energy in order to recover.

The theme of this religious gathering was based on John 8, verse 12: "Muri umucyo w'isi, Muri umunyu w'isi': 'You yourself are the light of the world; you are the only one."

Delegations from various countries were represented: people from the Baganda-, Batanzania- and Bahima tribe as well as Rwandans (Hutus and Tutsis), Europeans and Americans. The meeting made a deep impression on me and inspired me deeply. It was really impressive to sing together, full of hope: 'Tukutendereza Yesu' ('Praise Jesus'). That moment, that song, inspired me so much that it heralded my first step towards reconciliation.

Also, I considered it a great experience to meet people from other parts of the world, representatives of other races and nationalities. We slept in the same room, shared meals with each other, exchanged experiences. We sang and danced together, moved in the same rhythm and we prayed, especially for Rwanda. In short, it was an inspiring, unforgettable time.

Inspired by the love of one's neighbour, the three of us decided to reflect on our genuine willingness to reconcile with other people. Our theme was: To walk in the love and light of God and to demonstrate His love by shining that love and that light in our lives. And when life is tasteless, we would be life's salt. Where darkness prevails, we must be the light. That would take effort and it would be painful. But we saw these as important components of reconciliation. With this theme, we returned to Rwanda where we needed to put our theme into practice in everyday life. If you reconcile, you can truly experience what it means to be comforted by God. But it becomes even more meaningful when you can offer consolation to others.

During our stay in Kenya we received a message from God - it looked like a vision - that all three of us would travel to different countries. Just as we saw the Nile and the railway for the first time in Kenya, so we would visit other countries as well. Years later this vision would become a reality for all three of us.

In 2004, I arrived in Europe for the first time when I visited Germany with Solace Ministries. Our group consisted of:
- Jean Gakwandi, founder and director of the organisation;
- Emmanuël Ngoga, a former esteemed member;
- Henriëtte Sebera, a former board member; and
- myself, Mama Lambert, in charge of Solace Ministries' counselling department.

We were invited by Wolfgang Reinhardt to shed some light on the activities of Solace Ministries and to share our testimonies for audiences in Germany. We were warmly and hospitably received and were given the opportunity to visit several big cities, such as Berlin, Leipzig, Dresden and Kassel.

Here I took the second step on my road to reconciliation, by listening to and revisiting my views of another continent concerning the genocide in Rwanda.

I happened to have still been wondering why the international community had not done anything to prevent the violent bloodshed and had not intervened to end the genocide in all those months. All the more so because the people who had fled Rwanda by plane must have recounted the terrible crimes as eyewitnesses.

Also, people in ultimate despair wrote or phoned abroad to ask for urgent help. Unfortunately, those desperate cries for help were not heard. Through my visits abroad I gained more insight on the commitment and compassion of people in other countries in relation to Rwanda during and after the genocide.

In 2011, I received an invitation from Anne-Marie de Brouwer and her partner Freek Dekkers to come to the Netherlands. Anne-Marie is a committed woman with her heart in the right place. She wrote, together with Sandra Ka Hon Chu, the book cited earlier: 'The Men Who Killed Me: Rwandan Survivors of Sexual Violence.'

Anne-Marie and Sandra tackled a taboo by sharing the testimonies of sixteen Rwandan women and a man who were horribly victimized by rape.

Anne-Marie not only wrote a book, she also co-founded with Freek the Mukomeze foundation. 'Mukomeze' can be translated as: 'Empower her.' Their foundation supports genocide survivors of sexual violence through individual sponsorships and projects, including in the areas of education and agriculture, so that women can generate income. The Mukomeze foundation partners with Solace Ministries.

My reception in the Netherlands was fantastic. I really felt at home. Not only was I given the chance to tell the board of Mukomeze (Anne-Marie, Freek, Marie-José Hoefnagel, Annemarie Middelburg, Eefje de Volder and Pinar Okur) more about my work at Solace Ministries, but I also had the opportunity to do so at the Lucas Church in Tilburg and at the Rotary Club in Vught.

I also visited the National Monument Camp Vught, where many innocent people were imprisoned by the Germans during the Second World War.

I also went to Haarlem to visit the home of Corrie ten Boom. She was an inspiring Christian woman who, during the Second World War, hid people in her house who were sought by the German occupiers. She was betrayed and arrested and sent to a concentration camp, but she survived the war.

What really spoke to me about Corrie was that she had met a camp guard some years after the war who asked her for forgiveness for what he had done to her and to many others. Corrie experienced inner conflict, but found the strength to forgive this man.

In March 2013, I travelled to the United States of America. Jean Gakwandi, his wife Viviane and I were invited by Carol Gumm to speak about forgiveness in Wisconsin. The theme of the gathering was: 'Every person has a history'. This journey had for me another remarkable experience in store: for the first time in my life I felt what it was like to be in a place with a temperature of -20 degrees Celsius.

In June 2013, I visited the Netherlands another time, again at the invitation of Anne-Marie and Freek. This time to write this book about my life, almost twenty years after surviving the genocide. Together with Hans Dekkers and Birgit Marres I worked a full month to record my story, so that Hans could write it down later. Recalling memories and looking back on my life was healing, but sometimes also very difficult, because all the pain for my lost loved ones re-emerged very intensely.

I visited National Monument Camp Vught again in June. I took part in a memorial ceremony to commemorate the transport of children, which took place from Camp Vught. Many children imprisoned in this camp were put on freight trains and transported to concentration camps in Germany and Poland. Few children returned alive. In National Monument Camp Vught, I was given the opportunity to honour all those innocent children, victims of a derailed system in which they were not welcome and thus killed during the war, just as my innocent children were killed during the genocide. I laid flowers at the monument and expressed the wish that they rest in peace and that we would see each other in heaven.

Children who read out loud the names of the victims seemed to be very aware of their peers' suffering. He who knows suffering, knows better than anyone how to abolish suffering. Those who deny the genocide are preaching oblivion. To prevent a violent future, it is important to continuously remember the past.

I also visited the Anne Frank House in Amsterdam. Anne Frank is a 14-year old Jewish girl and a symbol of the victims of the Holocaust that took place during World War II in which six million Jews were exterminated in gas chambers and camps. In 1942, Anne and her family had been hiding for two years in a concealed annex. Eventually they were betrayed and deported to a concentration camp, where Anne died. Her diary 'The Secret Annexe', which was found after the war, is known all over the world.

I also had the opportunity to speak before the Saint Laurentiuschurch of Ulvenhout, in collaboration with Diny Peters and Ad van Bijnen. I spoke to the worshippers about forgiveness and reconciliation. The musical part of the ceremony was provided by a Gregorian choir 'Schola Karolus Magnus' from Nijmegen, who sang beautiful songs of hope and consolation. The theme was 'Virgin-Marters' and dealt with the painful abuse of women since time immemorial. During the service we also prayed for Mukomeze, Solace Ministries, widows and orphans, the poor, the whole world and in particular for Rwanda and my deceased family members.

Law philosopher Professor Bert van Roermund from Tilburg University interviewed me in the synagogue in Tilburg and after this interview, there was a commemorative ceremony to honour all genocide victims of 1994. The ceremony was attended by guest of honour the Ambassador of Rwanda in the Netherlands, his Excellency Sir Jean Pierre Karabaranga. Also present were students of the university and Rwandan friends in the Netherlands who had played an important role in organizing that day, Alphonse Muleefu and Felix Ndahinda.

In April 2014 I was again in the Netherlands, now at the invitation of the 'Institute of Social Studies' in The Hague to speak during the twentieth commemoration of the genocide: 'Kwibuka 20 remember-unite-renew'. During this gathering, several other people also spoke about remembering, uniting and renewing, amongst which were Dutch former minister Jan Pronk and our ambassador, his Excellency Sir Jean Pierre Karabaranga.

In February 2015 my daughter Denise married Boyd, an Australian man, in Kigali. Man proposes, God disposes. How things can happen in the world. The genocidaires wanted to exterminate us, but it did not fit in God's plan that Denise, Lambert, Dieudonné and I would be killed. Furthermore, I could never have guessed that my daughter would marry an Australian man. The wedding day was a memorable and very festive day.

In April 2015, I visited the Netherlands for the fourth time, this time at the invitation of 'Academic Forum' and the Christian student union 'Veritas Forum', both of Tilburg University. I spoke about justice and forgiveness during the symposium 'It's Not Fair' and described how I dealt with these two themes in my life after the horrors of the genocide. More than three hundred students and other interested people attended the symposium. The ambassador of Rwanda in the Netherlands, his Excellency Sir Jean Pierre Karabaranga, was also present.

While I had initially express my doubts about the role of the international community during the genocide, my visits to Kenya, Germany, the United States of America and the Netherlands unreservedly illustrated that outside Rwanda there are many people who are with us in their thoughts and that a number of them also turned their empathy into concrete support.

For me this emphasized once more the importance of reconciliation with people in other countries, and it gave me hope that the genocide would never happen again, because young people everywhere said unconditionally: "This can never happen again!"

Below tall eucalyptus trees goes a broad, quiet sand road to Nyanza. Looking over the hills, from the top where I used to live, a memorial can be found on the side of the road, near the place where the infamous barricade 'Progrès' was situated. Here my five murdered children are buried: Joyeuse, Claudette, Germain, Olivier and Rutayisire. Their names, together with nine others, are inscribed at the top of the white memorial stone. It reads: 'Urwibutso rw'inzirakarengane zazize itsembabwoko ryo mu 1994' or 'Remember the innocent victims: reject the senseless killing of 1994'.

I have come to the conclusion that with genuine reconciliation, I closed a cycle that began with the terrible events of 1994, events with traumatic consequences.
Counselling showed me the way to healing, to light and hope. A very long way, but a way in which - for me - the sun rose again at the end of it, and a new future was ahead.
Inspiring support, true forgiveness and genuine reconciliation have been the feeding powers that have blossomed from my disfigured life.

My past, present and future can be found in these hopeful words of Job: "Because for a tree there is hope. If it's cut down, it will grow new shoots that will develop into branches. Although its roots in the ground are old and the trunk will slowly die, it will grow and flourish again as a young tree as soon as it receives water."

*The memorial at 'Progrès' in Nyanza district,
where my children are laid to rest.*

*We have not all been killed during the genocide. With (from left to right):
Claudine (a daughter of good friends), Lambert, Sylvie (my sister-in-law)
and her little daughter Liliane, Dieudonné, Françoise and Denise.*

Denise Uwimana (second left), Droscella Nduwimana (fourth left) and I (fifth left) in Kenya in 2000, where we received God's promise that we would travel.

Wolfgang Reinhardt invited us in 2004 in Germany to speak about the work of Solace Ministries. With (from left to right): Emmanuël Ngoga, Wolfgang Rienhardt, Henriëtte Sebera, unknown, Jean Gakwandi and myself.

In 2011, during my first visit to the Netherlands, I spoke, amongst other places, in the Lucas church in Tilburg.

*In 2013 we were invited by Carol Gumm in
the United States of America to speak about forgiveness.
With (from left to right): myself, Viviane Mukamuseruka and Jean Gakwandi.*

*My second visit to the Netherlands, in 2013, was dedicated to writing this book,
together with Hans Dekkers and Birgit Marres.*

During my second visit to the Netherlands I was able to share my testimony in the church of Ulvenhout. With (from left to right): myself, Freek Dekkers, pastor Piet van Gorp and Dini Peters.

In 2013 I spoke during the genocide commemoration organised by Tilburg University in the Synagoge in Tilburg. With Bert van Roermund and myself.

Wreath laying at the Children's Memorial at National Monument Camp Vught in 2013. Commemorating the innocent children who had been held here during the Second World War and were deported.

In 2014 I spoke in The Hague at the Institute of Social Studies within the context of the twentieth commemoration of the genocide against the Tutsi. (photo: ISS The Hague)

Wedding of my daughter Denise and her husband Boyd on 14 February 2015. 'Man proposes, God disposes.' With (from left to right): myself, Boyd, Denise, Lambert and Dieudonné.

In April 2015 I spoke in front of an audience of about three hundred people on justice and forgiveness during a symposium organised at Tilburg University in the Netherlands, in the presence of his Excellency Sir Jean Pierre Karabaranga, the Ambassador of Rwanda. (photo: igihe)

On September 29th, 2015, I graduated for my study theology at RIET. With (from left to right): Father Nathan Ndyamiyemenshi (rector RIET and supervisor of my thesis), myself, Father André Mfitumukiza (president of the jury), Cyprien Kwibeshya and Beatrice Mujawingoma.

GLOSSARY

AIDS
A syndrome (Acquired Immune Deficiency Syndrome*)* which occurs as a result of damage to the human immune system, caused by the Human Immunodeficiency Virus (HIV). The term AIDS is applied to the most advanced stages of HIV infection.

ARV
Also known as 'antiretroviral treatment'. This is a treatment for people living with HIV, and fights HIV by stopping or interfering with the reproduction of the virus in the body, reducing the amount of virus in the body.

Bourgmestre
Term used in 1994 to refer to the leader of a 'commune'. The bourgmestre, or mayor, was the most powerful person in the 'commune' and fell under the authority of a prefect.

Commune
A local authority or community.

Conseiller
Head of a sector, a part of a 'commune'.

FAR
Forces Armées Rwandaises, Rwanda's official army, before and during the genocide.

Gacaca
Kinyarwanda for 'on the grass'. Gacaca tribunals were Rwanda's traditional law courts. Their mandate expanded after 1994, allowing them to pass judgement over crimes committed during the genocide.

Genocidaire
A person guilty of planning genocide or contributing to its execution.

Genocide
The deliberate and systematic extermination, complete or partial, of an ethnic, racial, religious or national group. The term was first used in the 1948 UN Convention on the Prevention and Punishment of the Crime of Genocide.

Habyarimana
Habyarimana was a general in the army until 1973 and in that year he staged a coup and proclaimed himself the new president of Rwanda. The continuing conflict between Hutus and Tutsis, with many deaths (mainly Tutsi) led to a UN resolution requiring Habyarimana to take a more democratic course. In 1993, an accord was reached between the conflicting parties in Arusha (Tanzania). On one of the return flights in April 1994, the aircraft in which president Habyarimana was travelling was shot down above Kigali, which set in motion the genocide.

HIV
See AIDS. A person who has been diagnosed with HIV is referred to as a person living with HIV.

Inkotanyi
Kinyarwanda term, used by Hutu extremists to refer to the members of the Tutsi liberation front (RPF) in Uganda. They also used this term to refer to suspected Tutsi spies.

Interahamwe
Kinyarwanda term translated as 'those who attack together'. A paramilitary movement consisting mainly of Hutu youths who stirred up violence against Tutsis during the genocide.

Inyenzi
'Cockroach' in Kinyarwanda. Hutus frequently used this term of abuse to insult Tutsis.

Kayibanda
The first president of Rwanda after the declaration of independence in 1962. Despite the bloody violence of Hutus towards Tutsis in the preceding years, the first elections were held in 1961 and the Hutu party MDR Parmehutu of Kayibanda won by an absolute majority.

Kinyarwanda
The national language of Rwanda.

MDR Parmehutu
Democratic Republican Movement-party of the movement for the emancipation of the Hutus. This was the political party of president Kayibanda, the first president of Rwanda.

MRND
National-Revolutionary Movement for Development. As of 1975 this was the only political party that was allowed in Rwanda, led by president Habyarimana.

Population groups in Rwanda
Rwanda had three ethnic population groups. The largest group at 85 percent of the population was the Hutus, followed by the Tutsis at around 10 percent and the Twas (pygmy people) at around 5 percent. In the 1930s, Belgium, then colonial ruler of Rwanda, imposed mandatory registration on the population, obliging all inhabitants to state which ethnic group they belonged to. Ethnic background was also specified on one's identity card. This made it easy for the Hutus to draw up lists of Tutsis before and during the genocide. Nowadays, people only speak of Rwandans.

Prefect and prefecture
In 1994 Rwanda was divided into 12 prefectures, each headed by a prefect. Until the genocide, Mama Lambert lived in the prefecture of Gitarama. Since 2006, the 12 prefectures were replaced by 5 provinces.

Presidential Guard
Elite troops of the president of Rwanda.

RPF
'Rwandan Patriotric Front' or 'Front Patriotique Rwandais'. This was a political and military movement started in 1987 by Tutsi refugees in Uganda. From as early as 1950, Rwandan Tutsis fled to Uganda to escape the ethnic cleansing. In 1994, the RPF invaded Rwanda and ended the genocide. At the time, the RPF was under the command of Paul Kagame, now president of Rwanda. The RPF is now the ruling political party.

RTLM
'Radio Télévision Libre des Mille Collines': a station managed by Hutus, notorious for hateful anti-Tutsi propaganda before and during the genocide.

Rwandan franc
Rwanda's official currency.

Serpent
Snake; term of abuse used by Hutus for Tutsis.

Solace Ministries
An aid organisation founded soon after the genocide in Kigali by Jean Gakwandi, himself a survivor. The aim of the organisation is to offer comfort and help to widows, orphans, and people living with HIV or AIDS, all victims of the genocide. The institution started out as a small group, but grew over the years into a large aid organisation that provides services throughout Rwanda. Mama Lambert has been head of Counselling at Solace Ministries since 2002.

Zone Turquoise
During the genocide a 'safe zone' established by the French in the southwest of Rwanda. In this period, the French were accused of having helped the perpetrators of the genocide escape via this zone to Congo.

ACKNOWLEDGEMENTS

First and foremost I am thankful to God for His protection ever since I was born, especially in 1959, 1963, 1973, 1990 and 1994. Glory be to God!

Special thanks goes to Anne-Marie de Brouwer and Freek Dekkers for opening their home to me. This book would certainly never have been written without their help.

I would like to thank Hans and Ria Dekkers. They are such great models of patience for me. Their effort and encouragement helped make this book possible.

How can I begin to explain the effort and encouragement afforded me by Hans Dekkers and a courageous woman named Birgit Marres? Hans made this book possible by writing it all down. Birgit helped me with the translation while I told my story.

I would like to especially thank Hans Dekkers from the very bottom of my heart. He felt my pain and suffering while writing my story. It was by no means easy to hear and record my life story; it was emotional, shocking and exhausting. I am deeply touched by his patience and support. He worked countless days and nights on this book, for which I am very grateful. This book would not have been possible without him.

I would also like to thank the publisher, Wolf Legal Publishers, in particular Willem-Jan van der Wolf, who believed in this book from the very beginning. Thank you also to Ditty Vos for designing and formatting this book.

A special heartfelt thanks goes to the people who translated this book from Dutch to English and whom were found through the organisation Translation Without Borders: Joseph Braddock, Margaret Wesseling, Anna Asbury and Lydia Heilmann. They dedicated their free time to translating the many chapters of this book, even on a second occassion after some alterations were made to the Dutch version of the book. I also sincerely thank Sandra Ka Hon Chu who was in charge of the final editing of the English version of this book. Their time and dedication is beyond words. Having the book available in multiple languages helps me to share my story to many people all over the world.

Many thanks to all those who said they would pray for this book: Jean Gakwandi and Viviane Mukamuseruka, Carol Gumm and Ray's family, Laurie Hendrickson's family, Julie Klosiewski's family, Dele Mosaku, Sigi Manthey, Remi Obanjoko, Emmanuël and Mary Ngoga, Nicolas and Elsie Hitimana, Drocella Nduwimana, Dusabe Cesarie, Colette Mukandoli, Denise Uwimana, Fred Mulisa and Candida Mukabarere.

I thank the survivors in my family, namely the families of: Innocent Habimana, Sylvie Uwamaliya, Bienvenue Emile Havugimana, Fani and Claude Habyalimana, Rosine and Patrick Sharangabo, Venantie Kamaraba and Aloys Gahamanyi.

A special word of thanks goes to the board members of the Mukomeze Foundation in the Netherlands, Solace Ministries in Rwanda and Kwizera Ministries in the United States. I will never forget your love and solace.

I am thankful for the strong faith of Donald and Lorna Miller, as it was of great support to me during the production of this book as well as in my daily life. Thank you for sharing your testimonies, which gave me so much encouragement.

Finally I would like to thank all my friends and those who God sent in my service, who stood by me and helped me. As a result, I am now able to do the same for others; those who have suffered or are still suffering from the same pain which I suffered. Now I can comfort others, particularly widows and orphans, because of the support that I received from friends.

God bless you all!

Mama Lambert

When I heard Mama Lambert's very special story and was invited to write about her life, I saw it as an honour, which is why I accepted.

Though the barbaric tyranny that Mama Lambert experienced, and above all the absolutely amazing manner in which she dealt with her fate, she is a true example and a source of inspiration for me and I hope for everyone who reads this book.

Many wonderful people helped to make this book a reality. I mention here:

Birgit Marres was our passionate and capable interpreter, who translated French-Rwandan directly into Dutch every day during the weeks that we sat listening to Mama Lambert's life story. She also contributed some very useful ideas during the drafting of this book.

Then there's my son, Freek, who spent so much time critically analyzing the text as a 'neutral' reader. His edits and valuable comments helped contribute to the book's readability.

Thank you to Anne-Marie de Brouwer who asked me to write this book; she was the contact person for Mama Lambert and devoted the necessary time to be my liaison and editor, and carried out all the background work to orchestrate the completion and publication of this book.

I would like to sincerely thank them all for their very amicable and valuable assistance.

Hans Dekkers

ABOUT THE AUTHORS

Mama Lambert (1952)
Mama Lambert's birth name is Beata Mukarubuga. A Rwandan Tutsi, she worked as a primary school teacher before the genocide. She survived the 1994 genocide against the Tutsis, in which she lost her husband and five of her eight children. Since the genocide, she calls herself Mama Lambert, 'the mother of Lambert'. Mama Lambert lives in Kigali and since 2002 has held a permanent position with Solace Ministries, an organisation founded in 1995 on behalf of widows, orphans and people with HIV or AIDS who survived the genocide. Mama Lambert works as head of the counselling department. In 2015, she successfully completed a degree in theology at the Rwanda Institute of Evangelical Theology (RIET). She has visited several countries and has spoken of her experiences. In 2013, Mama Lambert visited the Netherlands for several weeks to tell her story.

Hans Dekkers (1946)
For many years Hans Dekkers worked as a primary school teacher and headmaster in the Netherlands. Hans studied Dutch at the Katholieke Leergangen in Tilburg. He is married with two children. He learned about Rwanda through his son Freek and his life partner Anne-Marie de Brouwer, founders of the Dutch Mukomeze Foundation, which works closely with Solace Ministries. Hans visited Rwanda in 2007 and 2014 and learned more about modern-day life in the country and the consequences of the genocide. Hans wrote down Mama Lambert's life story.

Solace Ministries

Solace Ministries is a non-governmental organisation in Rwanda with the aim of supporting survivors of the 1994 genocide against the Tutsis. Jean Gakwandi, himself a survivor of the genocide, is the founder and director of Solace Ministries.

In particular, the organisation supports widows, orphans and women who were raped during the genocide, many of whom were infected with HIV. Solace Ministries strives to meet the needs of the genocide survivors holistically, by supporting them with physical, psychological, material, socio-economic and spiritual care. Mama Lambert works as head of the Counselling department.

Solace Ministries cooperates with several national and international partners.

For further information on Solace Ministries, see: www.solacem.org.